French

Gina Butler, B.A.

Published by Intercontinental Book Productions
in conjunction with Seymour Press Ltd.

Distributed by Seymour Press Ltd.,
334 Brixton Road, London, SW9 7AG

Published 1977 by Intercontinental Book Productions, Berkshire House, Queen Street, Maidenhead, Berks, SL6 1NF in conjunction with Seymour Press Ltd.

1st edition, 5th impression 1.81.5
Copyright © 1977 Intercontinental Book Productions
Made and printed by Spottiswoode Ballantyne Ltd,
Colchester and London
ISBN 0 85047 912 6

Contents

Introduction:
   Preparing for the examination, 7

Oral examination, 9

Dictation, 23

Translation into English, 31

Translation into French, 45

Comprehension, 56

Essay, 72

The examination paper, 87

Acknowledgement: The publisher would like to thank the University of Cambridge Local Examinations Syndicate for their permission to reproduce their exam questions on pages 15, 23 and 34.

Introduction:
Preparing for the examination

Whether we like it or not, exams still represent the culmination of a period of study and are used as a measure of achievement. Arguments about the merits or otherwise of such a system are not our concern here. This book sets out (a) to show that exam performance can be improved by practice and analysis, and (b) to provide the potential O-level candidate with opportunities to better not only his exam technique, through practice of the exercises he is likely to face, but also his awareness of what is being tested in those exercises, through analysis of the elements which characterise good and bad scripts. The book should, therefore, be used as a teaching tool – the student should be able to identify from each chapter certain techniques appropriate to each type of exercise, and his task is to apply these, first to the examples presented, and subsequently to the course work he is engaged upon. Each chapter outlines procedures which are meant to organise logically the student's approach to the exam: this in turn should enable him to work economically and (it is hoped) profitably at the time of the exam. For this reason the **common feature of all chapters except the first** in the book is the **check-list**. For the oral exam it is not possible to provide a check-list, of course, since what you say has then 'gone for ever', but experience has shown that if you are in the habit of carefully checking such areas as verb and subject agreement in your written work, then it will stand you in good stead in the oral examination.

It would be monotonous to provide a topic guide for each chapter, since it simply is not possible to separate areas of learning in this way. Throughout **you are being tested on your total linguistic competence**, therefore the whole range of your level of experience is 'the topic' in each paper of the exam. You cannot escape verbs or pronouns or whatever you find particularly difficult, in the hope that this year they will not be tested. You cannot form language without them. So – be prepared!

These are the areas in which you should be truly competent if you are to consider yourself exam-ready:
Tense forms and usage This will include not only endings and straightforward equivalents, but also nuances of meaning (between 'je mangerai' and 'je vais manger', for instance, both

of which express a future idea). It also embraces the interaction of all tenses (particularly imperfect, perfect and past historic) and the many verbal constructions, (e.g. avant de + infinitive).

Pronouns They come in all shapes and sizes, and you should be able to recognise them in use, and to use them all with confidence in your own writing.

Conjunctions, adverbs, prepositions (including their idiomatic use), and **common idioms** form a staple O-level diet. These, along with vocabulary areas (which are compounded from the words and phrases most frequently found in French today) are to be learned from most text books. You should be particularly careful not to neglect points such as idioms involving 'faire' and 'avoir', and those examiners' pets – the 'depuis', 'il y a . . .', 'venir de . . .' constructions.

It is no use any student thinking he can learn this subject all at the last minute. Language learning is not an instant process and if you have been less than diligent in the past, you will not be able to achieve miracles in the weeks before the exams. That does not mean to say that you should not systematically plan your revision – indeed you should. Beginning with areas you may be weak in, you should **thoroughly and unhurriedly go through your own notes or grammar book**, and see that you are entirely in command of the material. One major area in one week is quite enough and you should therefore plan to **begin your serious revision** at least **three months** before the examination period. You are much more likely to absorb it properly that way. As far as **vocabulary** and **idioms** are concerned, you should start at the beginning of the fifth year revising small areas at a time (e.g. colours, animals, clothing and so on). Four or five idiomatic phrases a week are ample if you begin this process in good time. You must have time to practise using them, after all.

Just as a final word, let it be said that for the really good candidate, who has been conscientious over the whole period of language study, there will in fact be little to learn before the exam, apart from additional vocabulary. The closer you can come to this ideal approach, the easier the whole experience will be, and the more likely you are to do well.

In any case – *BONNE CHANCE!*

GINA BUTLER, who obtained her degree at the University of London, has taught in France as well as in Britain where she has held posts in schools, language centres and colleges of education. She was head of the Faculty of Modern Languages at Codsall Comprehensive School and is at present Deputy Headmistress of Highfields School, Wolverhampton, and an examiner in French at Ordinary Level. She is the author of *French for the Businessman II* (Interlang), and of the Key Facts *GCE O-Level Passbook: French*.

key facts

Model Answers

BIOLOGY, R. Whitaker, B.Sc. and
J. M. Kelly, B.Sc.

CHEMISTRY, C. W. Lapham, M.Sc.

ENGLISH, Keith Linley, M.A.

GEOGRAPHY, R. Knowles, M.A.

HISTORY (Social and Economic, 1815–1939),
M. C. James, B.A.

MODERN MATHEMATICS, A. J. Sly, B.A.

PHYSICS, D. F. Erskine, B.Sc.

As illustrations of both good and poor work, genuine
student answers to examination questions have been
included in each book in the *Model Answers* series. These
student answers, which may contain errors, have been
placed inside boxes wherever they occur, to distinguish
them from the main body of the text.

Model Answers

Oral examination

The oral examination takes place before the period of the written papers and is conducted either by a visiting examiner (an averagely sane and understanding person), who is just as anxious as you are that the whole experience should be a success, or by your own teacher, who may also possess the above personal qualities, and who will probably have a tape recorder to record your interview for later marking.

In this part of the exam you **must**, quite literally, **earn every mark by positive effort**. A combination of two factors will provide the formula for good marks – not only **reasonable spoken French** but also **willingness on your part to speak!** It cannot be over-emphasised just how important to the outcome is your own approach. Everyone makes allowances for candidates' nervousness, but lack of effort or broody silence obviously wastes time and patience. As with any other interview, a positive attitude can only bring you credit. A smile creates a good impression and costs nothing.

Over recent years the oral exam has assumed an increasing importance in the total mark, and, thankfully, this is likely to be the pattern of the future, too. It reflects the greater part played by comprehension and verbal communication skills in the learning of a foreign language nowadays. Some or all of the following exercises will feature in your exam.

Reading aloud (possibly with comprehension questions);

General questions (unprepared) *OR* **prepared questions;**

Conversation on specific topics;

Description of a picture or series of pictures (selected and prepared by candidates in advance);

Role-play

For obvious reasons a realistic oral examination is difficult to simulate in written form, and since the oral is in any case impromptu to a large extent, and may last up to fifteen minutes per candidate, extracts and guidelines only can be given here.

Model answer

We will assume that the candidate has a reading passage to prepare (not reproduced here), general questions to answer, a picture to describe, and a role to play in a given situation.

Candidate no. 359   Susan Davies
Bonjour Mademoiselle. Votre numéro est bien le 359 ?
Oui, Monsieur.
Et comment vous appelez-vous, Mademoiselle ?
Je m'appelle Susan Davies.
Quel âge avez-vous, Susan ? J'ai seize ans.
Et avez-vous des frères ou des soeurs ? Non, je suis enfant unique.
Cela vous plaît d'être enfant unique ?
Pas du tout; j'aimerais avoir un frère plus âgé que moi, pour m'aider avec la vaisselle !
Combien de temps vous faut-il pour venir à l'école ?
Il me faut une demi-heure.
Et après le travail de l'école, que faites-vous comme loisirs ?
J'aime le sport, surtout la natation – et aussi la musique. Je fais partie d'un groupe folklorique. L'année dernière nous sommes allés à un festival de musique.
Parlez-moi de cela.
C'était au pays de Galles. Nous avons passé trois jours là-bas, et nous avons rencontré des groupes anglais et étrangers.
De quels pays venaient-ils ?
Oh, de la France, de l'Allemagne, de l'Amérique aussi.
Et cela vous a coûté cher ?
Non, nous avons décidé de faire du camping, donc nous avons dû faire la cuisine nous-mêmes – et nous avons fait le voyage en autostop.
Que ferez-vous cet été ?
Nous n'avons pas encore décidé. Peut-être irons-nous en Ecosse.

A l'école, quelles sont vos matières préférées ?
J'aime l'anglais, l'histoire – le français aussi, mais je n'aime pas les mathématiques.
Comptez-vous rester en Sixth Form ?
Oui, je crois. Cela dépendra des résultats des examens !
Que ferez-vous si vous restez à l'école ?
Je ferai l'anglais et l'histoire probablement.
Et que ferez-vous plus tard ?
Je voudrais être journaliste, mais on m'a dit que c'est une vie difficile.
Eh bien, bonne chance. Que feriez-vous si vous aviez un an de vacances et beaucoup d'argent ?
Je ferais le tour du monde ; j'aimerais voir des endroits intéressants (comme le Japon) et rencontrer les gens des autres pays.
Comment feriez-vous ce voyage ?
Surtout par avion, mais aussi en bâteau et peut-être en scooter.
Très bien. Maintenant passons à l'image devant vous. Où se passe cette scène ? (See page 12.)
Elle se passe dans une gare. Il y a un train au quai numéro un qui partira bientôt pour Nice.
Que font les gens que vous voyez sur l'image ?
Quelques-uns sont déjà montés dans le train ; d'autres n'y sont pas encore montés. Il y a un monsieur qui va peut-être manquer le train – il court pour l'attraper. Il est encombré de ses paquets.
Imaginez ce que les passagers ont fait avant de monter dans le train.
Ils ont peut-être acheté des journaux ou des revues au kiosque qui se trouve à gauche, et avant de faire cela, ils ont dû acheter leurs billets.
Décrivez le monsier près du kiosque.
C'est un vieil homme aux cheveux blancs et avec une moustache. Il a l'air confus.
A quoi sert un bureau de renseignements ?
A fournir des détails sur les horaires et le prix des voyages.
Bon. Maintenant vous devez jouer le rôle indiqué sur la fiche.

Role-play situation
A lost pair of gloves
1. *You return to a shop where you think you have lost your gloves. Tell the manager you were shopping in his store about an hour ago, and now find you have lost your gloves.*
2. *When he asks, say you were shopping in the toy department.*
3. *They were green wool gloves.*
4. *Some have been found. Decide whether they are yours.*

12

Bonjour Mademoiselle. Comment est-ce que je peux vous être utile?

Bonjour Monsieur. Je faisais quelques courses dans votre magasin il y a une heure à peu près, et maintenant je ne peux pas trouver mes gants. Je pense que je les ai perdus ici.

Vous avez fait des achats partout dans le magasin?

Non, je ne suis allée qu'au rayon des jouets. J'ai voulu acheter un cadeau pour l'anniversaire de mon petit neveu.

Et vous avez trouvé quelque chose de convenable?

Oui, je lui ai acheté un train électrique.

Vos gants, comment étaient-ils?

Ils étaient verts, et en laine. Ils étaient assez neufs.

Nous avons trouvé une paire de gants – les voilà.

Ah bon, oui – ce sont les miens. Je vous remercie beaucoup. Au revoir, Monsieur.

Au revoir, Mademoiselle.

Answer plan

Since most of this part of the examination is 'off-the-cuff', it is not so much a question of planning your answer at the time of the exam, but of sound preparation beforehand. It is essential to be in the right frame of mind to make the most of the time allotted to you – here there is no opportunity to revise your work. You should remember that the exam is not a quiz game; it is testing your oral ability in straightforward situations which relate to your everyday life (family, school life, interests, ambitions, daily routines, etc.). It aims to find out what you *do* know, not what you do not. The onus, therefore, is on you to show this. You will almost certainly have the opportunity to move away from a stereotyped question-and-answer situation to talk about something which interests you or is interesting about you. The examiner will be only too pleased to meet a candidate who shows some initiative, so it is only sensible to practise (in general terms – no speeches) what you might say on that subject. Look up relevant vocabulary, use your teacher's brain! If, however, you have a hobby but do not bother to prepare in this way and it comes up in the exam, then you will, in the first place, look and feel silly and, in the second, indicate to the examiner that you are probably a rather idle, off-hand character. That impression might just serve to upset his understanding and tolerant approach to you, but it would be entirely your own fault. Of course you may forget a vital word, you may genuinely not know something rather specialised, or not have made up your mind yet about a decision, but in these cases there are procedures to follow. You will *not* (if you have any sense) sit looking miserable, while the examiner tries to decide if you are ill, hypnotised or plain stupid – he is not after all a mind-reader. You *will* produce a phrase or question appropriate to the nature of your difficulty. Every candidate should know the following:

– Je ne comprends pas (la question) = I do not understand ...
– Pardon Monseiur/Madame, comment dit-on en français ...? = Excuse me, how do you say ... in French? (This question will not, however, be appreciated if the word you are asking about is one you should know.)
– Je n'y ai jamais pensé = I've never thought about that.
– Je n'ai pas encore décidé = I've not made up my mind yet.
– Je crois que ... = I think that ...

The ubiquitous 'je ne sais pas' is categorically *not* an 'open sesame' to success. It should be avoided if at all possible, and used only if you mean to say 'I do not know that fact'. Even then you should try to make it sound less glib by adding, for instance, 'Je regrette, Monsieur/Madame, mais je ne sais pas, or 'Je ne sais pas au juste, mais je crois que ...' (if you are not quite sure of your facts). If you follow this advice you may gain some credit in spite of a lapse of memory or genuine ignorance; certainly, if you do not, you cannot hope to improve your image with the examiner. You must be prepared for follow-up questions put to you. 'Pourquoi?' is the most likely. To answer 'Je ne sais pas' is irritatingly feeble.

All this therefore points to **thorough pre-exam planning**. Some of it must be done on your own, and some will obviously be done through your teacher; however, one cannot escape the fact that in any average forty-minute period you personally are not likely to have a lot of individual oral practice. Much useful work can be done if you and a friend help each other, taking turns asking and answering questions, working out a role-play situation, describing a picture or reading aloud. Just one word of warning – avoid over-rehearsal, particularly where prepared topics are a part of the test. A robot-sounding candidate can only expect to gain credit for accuracy, and will certainly be penalised overall for lack of spontaneity, of true conversational ability, and probably for fluency and intonation weaknesses. Your conversation must sound natural.

Let us now take the planning you will be able to do in the ten- to fifteen-minute period you have immediately prior to the exam.

You are (let us suppose) handed a **reading passage**, a **role-play situation**, and a **picture**.

Reading test

*L'an dernier, je décidai de repeindre l'extérieur de ma petite maison
de campagne. J'allai donc chez le marchand de couleurs acheter de
la peinture.*
*– Avec 20 kilos vous aurez assez pour toute la maison, me dit-il.
Dans mon inexpérience je commençai par en renverser la moitié sur
moi. Quant à l'autre moitié je l'étendis en une couche deux fois
trop épaisse. Me trouvant bientôt à court de peinture, je retournai
chez le marchand en acheter encore 10 kilos. Mais il ne voulut pas
m'en donner davantage.*
*– On n'a jamais employé que 20 kilos pour peindre cette maison
aussi loin que remontent mes souvenirs, déclara-t-il. Comme j'ai
horreur du gaspillage, vous n'en aurez pas un gramme de plus. Je
dus faire plus de 50 kilomètres pour avoir mes 10 kilos supplé-
mentaires!*

(University of Cambridge Local Examinations Syndicate)

Read it slowly to yourself to grasp the general meaning. Now
read it again, aloud, not too quickly and bearing in mind that
the passage does make sense! Remember particularly **intonation
and expression** (two major areas where candidates are criticised
severely by examiners). These features, together with clear diction
and good pronunciation, of course, are those which count.
Basic rules of intonation are: raise your voice at commas or
at the end of a phrase; drop it at the end of a sentence.
Basic rules of stress on individual words are: all syllables are
given similar weighting; in long words the last syllable alone has
particular stress, all others being equal, e.g. in/ex/pé/ri/*ence* is
composed of four equally weighted and one slightly stressed
last syllable. This is easy with practice and effort, even with
words which are very close to English in their spelling, and which
therefore need special care.

Pronunciation cannot suddenly be learned at this stage, but
again, if you try hard, you can achieve a reasonably authentic
standard. Words to pay particular attention to here would be
the one above, also 'supplémentaire', 'l'extérieur', 'la peinture',
'repeindre', 'gaspillage', and even 'kilomètres'.

Role-play situation

You are in a post-office.

1. *Ask the price of a stamp for a registered letter to England.*
2. *Say you would like three of one of the two different alternative rates proposed.*
3. *Ask if it is possible to post a parcel 15cm by 20cm on a Saturday afternoon.*
4. *Decide what to do in view of the answer you receive.*

You will see that you are frequently required to ask questions or initiate the conversation in some way. You must also expect to develop the situation further, depending on what line the examiner takes. **The role-play exercise is not a translation.** Your preparation must involve thinking out suitable expressions to render the basic skeleton situation described on the card. It must also involve projecting your imagination to possible extensions of the situation which the examiner may introduce. In this case minimal knowledge, as far as structure and vocabulary are concerned, must comprise:

'Quel est le prix de . . .?'; 'une lettre recommandée'; 'j'en voudrais . . .'; 'des timbres à . . . francs'; 'est-il possible de . . .?'; '15cm de long sur 20cm de large'.

Finally, but as important as much of the rest, do not forget to begin and end your conversation politely; 'Bonjour, Monsieur'; 'Merci et au revoir, Monsieur.' The French are great ones for polite formulae!

Description of a picture

Where there is a picture or series of pictures to describe, then you must prepare in just the same way. This exercise demonstrates your ability to use French in the same way as an essay does, at least in part. You cannot anticipate the examiner's questions, of course, but you can prepare yourself by considering:

(a) **physical aspect** of the people depicted (age, clothes, etc.);
(b) **actions** (not only what they *are* doing, but also what they have possibly just done (=venir de . . .), or what they might be going to do. Imagine it!);
(c) **location** (where people are in relation to others, or any buildings or other features of the picture).

The well known idioms which are used to express the kind of description suggested should be at your finger-tips, or rather tongue-tip, as should good phrases like 'à l'arrière-plan', 'au fond', etc. During your preparatory time look for ways in which you can involve a healthy variety of structure, vocabulary and tenses, (present tense only or principally gains very little credit). You must of course take your cue from the examiner, and **be especially alert to the tenses used in the questions** he asks. Vast numbers of candidates fritter away possible opportunities for gaining marks by failing to pick up the tense of the question, very often compounding their poor performance further by inventing an all-purpose, non-existent tense (of the type 'j'allé') which they randomly apply throughout. When he varies the tense in his questions the examiner is only trying to give you the opportunity of showing off your knowledge; he is not being devilish complicated and beastly in order to trap you. Some candidates are just too wrapped up in themselves and their anxieties to recognise this helping hand. Indulge yourself in whichever patent method will make you relaxed and able to pick up the examiner's linguistic signals, but **do not** be one of those foolish folk who forget all verb forms.

Student answer

Candidate no. 241   John Smith
(1) Votre numéro, c'est le 241, Monsieur ? Oui.
    Comment vous appelez-vous ? Je m'appelle John Smith.
    Et quel âge avez-vous, John ? J'ai seize ans.
    Vous avez des frères ou des soeurs ? Oui, un frère.
(2) Et quel âge a-t-il ? Il est treize.
(3) Comment venez-vous à l'école le matin ?
    Je arrive à huit heures et demie.
    Non, par quel moyen arrivez-vous à l'école ? en voiture ?
    en vélo ? Ah oui, à pied.
    Qu'est-ce que vous aimez faire après l'école, pendant les
    vacances ? Je fais le sport. Je joue au football pour
    l'école.
(4) Depuis combien de temps jouez-vous pour l'école ? Pour
    un an.
    Que ferez-vous l'année prochaine ? Je travaillerai dans
    une banque.
    Vous êtes fort en maths ? J'aime les mathématiques.
(5) Vous êtes jeune – parlons un peu de la vie de vos parents
    quand eux, ils étaient jeunes. Comment passaient-ils le
    temps ? Je ne sais pas.
    Il y avait la télévision à cette époque ? Non.
(6) Alors, que faisaient-ils ? Ils sont allés promener. Ils
    écouté à la radio.
(7) Où habitait votre père quand il était jeune ? En . . .
    Wales.
    Décrivez ce que vous avez fait ce matin avant de venir à

l'école. Je me suis levé, je me suis lavé, je me suis habillé, j'ai mangé des cornflakes et j'ai bu du thé.

(8) Et votre frère, s'est-il levé avant ou après vous? Il se lève avant . . . moi.

(9) Si vous n'étiez pas obligé de venir à l'école, comment passeriez-vous le temps? Je regarde la télévision, je joue au football.

(10) Et si vous étiez riche, qu'est-ce que vous aimeriez acheter? J'achèterais Raquel Welsh!

Euh! oui. Bon. Passons maintenant à l'image devant vous. Où est-ce que cette scène se passe? (See page 12.) A la gare.

(11) Décrivez un peu ce que font les personnes que vous voyez. Il y a des personnes dans le train, il y a des personnes sur le platform – oh, le quai.

Qui remarquez-vous surtout? Un vieux monsieur, et un homme avec beaucoup de paquets.

(12) Il est en retard, n'est-ce pas? Pourquoi? Il a missé l'autobus.

Où les passagers dans le train arriveront-ils enfin? A Nice.

Imaginez ce qu'ils ont fait avant de monter dans le train.

(13) Ils ont acheté un ticket – non, un billet.

(14) S'ils vont retourner à Paris par le train, quel genre de billet ont-ils pris? Un retour billet.

(15) Imaginez que ce monsieur-là vient de sortir du Bureau de Renseignements – qu'est-ce qu'il vient de faire là-bas? Il a demandé l'autre monsieur le temps pour le train.

(16) Que pourrait-on y faire aussi? Vous pouvez demander combien est le voyage.

Role-play situation

The Wrong Bus

You are travelling by bus and realise it is not the one you need.

1. Tell the conductor you think you have taken the wrong bus.

2. He will tell you in which direction the bus is travelling; say you wanted to go to the town centre.

3. Ask if it is the 72 bus you must take, and ask also if you can get off at the next stop.

Pardon, Monsieur, je crois ce n'est pas le bon autobus pour moi. Où va l'autobus?

> *Celui-ci, il va en direction de la gare.*
> Je veux aller au centre de la ville.
> *Alors oui, Monsieur, vous vous êtes trompé. Vous aimeriez savoir quel autobus prendre?*
> C'est le soixante-deux autobus je peux prendre?
> *Non, vous vous êtes trompé encore, c'est le soixante-douze.*
> Er . . . oui. Vous me permettez descendre à l'arrêt vient – non – à l'arrêt prochain.
> *Mais certainement, jeune homme.*

John Smith has not exactly covered himself in glory. But even with the limitations of his French he *could* have done better. He is obviously not interested in real conversation, and is not prepared to pretend he is. From the first section marked the tone is set: no concessions to recognised polite speech, but bald, telegram-style monosyllables or brief phrases. The moment the examiner hears a curt 'oui', he will have a fair inkling that John Smith is not going to be bending over backwards to converse. (It must be stated, however, that John Smith is by no means a really bad candidate – many are much worse.) The error in giving his brother's age reveals lack of practice in idiomatic forms other than the most basic. ('Il a treize ans' would be correct.)

(3) The question has been misunderstood, and serves to emphasise the need for thorough familiarity with common question forms. Football arouses a spark of interest and the candidate has actually volunteered some unsolicited information. If only there were more of this.

(4) The 'depuis' idiom is such a standard feature of O-level work that it really should cause no problem. As happens so often, it is the case here that if only the candidate had listened hard he would have discovered that the question supplies a great part of the answer. The rest of this section is acceptable, though the last question is not really answered.

(5) What a damp squib! John Smith has ignored the chance to use the imperfect tense, and has shown he has no great intention of using his imagination. Again he fails to add 'Monsieur' after 'non' and disregards the examiner's prompting.

(6) He is not the first to invent this verb; in any case he has plumped for the wrong tense (imperfect is indicated in the question), and in the second half has produced the favourite non-tense beloved of candidates. 'Ecouter', of course, always has a direct object.

(7) There is no excuse at all for not knowing 'au pays de Galles'.

(8) By his previous answer he has shown he can handle the perfect tense in well rehearsed situations, but has not thought before beginning to speak here. Tense and construction are the same; only the person of the verb needed adjustment.

(9) By concentrating on the question John Smith would have recognised the conditional tense – it certainly is not the present! (By the way it is dreadfully wearisome to hear endless variations on 'regarder la télé, écouter des disques, jouer au football' – are sixteen-year-olds really so boring?)

(10) At last! Candidate Smith is human after all!

(11) Here the candidate is using very elementary phrases and they are going to do him very little good. Compare this version with the earlier one describing the same scene. If you were the examiner how would you grade the two candidates on attitude and effort?

(12) This sort of blatant anglicised French makes an examiner cringe – by now John Smith has used up virtually all of his goodwill allowance.

(13) There would be no penalty here for correcting a mistake.

(14) 'Un billet aller-retour' should be standard fare at O-level – sorry for the pun, Mr Smith!

(15) This is full of errors of construction and vocabulary. 'Il a demandé à un monsieur l'heure du train.'

(16) A second conditional tense is not spotted. Does he mean 'How long is the journey?' or 'How much is the journey?' In either case 'est' conveys very little, just as 'il y a' does.

Role-play situation Taking wrong roads, buses, etc., happens fairly often in O-level French and so you should learn the right way to say it ('Je crois que je me suis trompé de . . .'). However, apart from the fact that a vital 'que' has been omitted, this attempt by John Smith is better than nothing. The question concerning the destination of the bus is rather blunt, but gets the message across!

Not for the first time tenses are confused. The present of 'vouloir' is not correct; 'je voulais' is needed.

In forming his next question our candidate has made numerous blunders:
(a) his number is wrong;
(b) he has not positioned it correctly in relation to the noun;
(c) again he has omitted the linking 'que', here a pronoun;
(d) he has confused 'devoir' and 'pouvoir'.

It so happens that because he has stuck too rigidly to translating each word as it comes along, he has not even hit upon the best (and easiest) way of saying the phrase: 'Est-ce que je dois . . .?' The weakness on verbal constructions seen earlier (15), is to be noted here, too, although he has made some effort to produce a pronoun. With his last phrase he was nearly there and had obviously tried to remember the right adjective.

All in all, John Smith has quite simply not made enough effort to earn positive marks. Quite apart from the obvious difference in standard between him and Susan Davies of the Model Answer, it is this factor which differentiates the two candidates most clearly. John's reluctance to say much unless pushed conveys eloquently enough his lack of interest. Granted that he has some weakness on tenses (but fewer than many others), he has never-theless done nothing to show off anything he might know. He could, even at this level of ability, have attempted a more varied sentence structure (clauses and pronouns are virtually non-existent). He has only introduced the most banal vocabulary. He has probably excused himself by saying 'I never was any good at French', but his standard could probably be average, and he could certainly give a better performance than this if he put his mind to it.

Common errors

On the question of **attitude**, it should be crystal clear by now that lack of determination to do the best one can is the chief fault of candidates. Looking pained or fixing the corner of the table with a forlorn, unblinking stare may be poetic poses but do no good in an oral examination.

On **spoken performance** the most common faults are either **mumbling** so that what you say cannot be heard, or (especially with the reading passage) **speaking too fast** so that you stumble over words and sound like a speeded-up record. In the first instance you cannot be given credit for what you **might** have said, and in the second you literally are rushing to penalise yourself. **Speak clearly and loudly enough** to be heard.

Lack of concentration on the precise question (especially the **tense of that question**) leads to many avoidable mistakes. The use of **'oui'**, **'non'**, **'je ne sais pas'** together with the **inability to formulate a sensible sentence indicating you**

have not understood are all pointers towards a weak candidate. The lack of preparation of the predictable elements of the exam (own family and self, etc.) is a further indicator of poor quality.

If you do not try and create for yourself the **maximum opportunity to develop a situation linguistically**, you will not earn marks. You should realise that in the picture you are describing, the man on the river bank fishing in the hot sun, the sleeping dog under the big tree . . . are there precisely in order that you should mention them all!

Examiners look for the **ability to recognise and handle** a variety of **tenses correctly**, the **ability to use pronouns** and **verb constructions confidently**, together with a **well-varied sentence structure**, containing a **range of vocabulary and idioms**. Mistakes with tenses and pronouns are among the most seriously penalised errors. Mistakes of gender (especially of common words) are also severely dealt with, as are mistakes of agreement ('le maison est grand', 'mon soeur est petit' are typical examples). Equally primitive errors concern those occasions when a preposition is contracted with an article, as in 'aux filles'. It is painful (and unprofitable!) to produce 'près de le magasin' et al.

It would be a great mistake to believe that fluency solves all problems. It simply is no use chattering away if what you are chattering on about is inaccurate. Indeed the candidate who goes on at great speed is very likely to produce those awful hybrid verb forms mentioned earlier in the chapter, and on many occasions the 'j'ai allé', 'nous avons tombé', 'il a prendu' type of error could quite possibly have been avoided if the candidate had slowed down somewhat and used the extra time to think out what he was going to say.

To sum up, it is in the oral exam that the candidate who has failed over the years to make a real effort to master the fundamental structures and to acquire a reasonable basic vocabulary will face most uncomfortably the stark reality of that situation. On the other hand, the oral examination can prove an enjoyable experience and is certainly one where it is in your interest not only to do your best, but also to be seen to be doing your best.

Dictation

Dictations have the uncompromising characteristic of being either right or wrong, and so in this chapter we shall simply offer as Model Answers two typical dictations from different Boards, as they are set out for the person conducting the examination, with phrase markings, but, in this case, with no liaison indications. Practise them with a friend as they stand; they also make useful reading passages. Take particular care over liaisons. Incidentally there are two isssues on which Examining Boards are divided in their practice. The first concerns the main narrative tense; depending on the Board this can be either past historic or perfect. Secondly it is the usual practice for proper names to be written on the blackboard beforehand, but this is not automatically the case. You should make sure you know what to expect from the Board you are working for.

Model answers

A. *Le concierge de chez nous | était un homme aimable | qui avait, | je crois, | entre cinquante et soixante ans. | Ses yeux étaient bleus, | ses cheveux blancs, | et il portait une petite barbe. | Il me souriait | toutes les fois | que je passais | devant sa loge. | Un jour, | cependant, | en sortant pour aller à l'école, | je ne le vis pas | à sa place habituelle. | Le soir, | quand je revins | vers cinq heures, | il n'était toujours pas là. | Je demandai à ma mère | s'il lui était arrivé | quelque chose. |*
'Il est tombé malade | la nuit dernière,' | me dit-elle. | 'On a dû | le transporter | à l'hôpital. | J'espère | que nous aurons bientôt | de bonnes nouvelles.'

(The Associated Examining Board)

B. *Mistaken Identity*
Madame Leclerc et son mari | venaient de s'installer | dans un bel appartement | au cinquième étage, | mais il y avait toujours | quelque chose qui ne marchait pas. | Ce jour-là | elle avait téléphoné | pour faire venir le plombier, | car elle n'arrivait pas à fermer | un des robinets | du lavabo. | Soudain | elle a entendu sonner. | Un monsieur un peu étonné | se tenait à la porte. | Elle l'a fait entrer, | et malgré ses protestations | elle l'a poussé ensuite | dans la salle de bain. | Mais enfin | il s'est écrié: |
– Je regrette, | madame, | mais cela ne me regarde pas. | Je suis

23

venu tout simplement | faire visite à un ami | qui demeure dans |
ce bâtiment, | et j'ai dû me tromper de numéro | en sonnant chez
vous. |

(University of Cambridge Local Examinations Syndicate)

Answer plan

A ransom note handed to a maid

(1) *La bonne, |* (2) *heureuse de voir |* (3) *qu'on ne l'avait pas oubliée |*
(4) *expliqua à Bernard |* (5) *et à l'inspecteur |* (6) *comment elle avait*
reçu | (7) *cette lettre : |*

– (8) *On a sonné |* (9) *vers trois heures. |* (10) *Je suis allée ouvrir |*
(11) *et un petit garçon |* (12) *a tendu une lettre. |* (13) *J'ai eu*
seulement le temps | (14) *d'examiner l'adresse |* (15) *et de re-*
connaître | (16) *l'écriture de mademoiselle, |* (17) *et il était parti ! |*

– (18) *Vous connaissez ce garçon ? |*

– (19) *Je ne l'ai jamais vu. |*

– (20) *Merci, vous pouvez sortir, |* (21) *dit Bernard à la domestique. |*
(22) *Alors, monsieur l'inspecteur, |* (23) *vous êtes encore |* (24) *dans*
le brouillard ? |

– (25) *Rassurez-vous. |* (26) *Cette lettre |* (27) *va nous mettre |*
(28) *demain matin |* (29) *en contact |* (30) *avec les bandits |* (31)
eux-mêmes. |

(Oxford and Cambridge Schools Examination Board)

First remember the title (which will be in English if there is one):
it will offer some clue as to the content. On the **first reading**
listen carefully to try and understand the passage as a whole
and the sequence of events. Here you should have little difficulty
in deducing that there is mystery afoot – an inspector has called
concerning a ransom note delivered by a small boy who darted
off almost immediately. If you correctly interpret 'bandits',
you should be quite confident about the gist of the story.

In the **second section** of this exam you are required to write the
passage as it is dictated in phrases. Each phrase is repeated
twice and as you normally have ample time to write the phrase
after the first hearing you should use the second as a first opportunity to check the sense and accuracy of what you have written.
Throughout you must bear in mind what has gone before, checking that verb forms and adjectival agreements particularly remain
consistent. For example, 'il mangeait' and 'ils mangeaient' are
identical in sound and only reference to the rest of the passage
will indicate the correct form.

There is no item of vocabulary or structure here which is beyond the experience of an O-level candidate. Whether or not you are able to distinguish and correctly transcribe the sounds you hear is a completely different matter, of course. Clearly candidates who are used to hearing and speaking French themselves are more likely to have success in doing this.

Let us now deal briefly with some difficulties which might face you here and suggest how you should go about resolving them.

(3) This is a phrase where the weak candidate will flounder, since it could sound like a single unending word, but as always, the application of logic and rules of syntax will sort out the difficulty. **'qu'on'** should figure high on the list of common spelling/sound combinations every candidate ought to have made for himself. It should not be necessary to spend time dwelling on the various spelling possibilities at the time of the exam. Taken from another point of view, the syntactical one, what else do you expect to follow **'voir'**? It has to be either a direct object or **'que'** + clause.

. . . 'ne l'avait pas oubliée'' Exactly as above, you should register that 'lavait' (for instance) can make no sense here, and so a direct object pronoun must be involved: further, this will indicate the pluperfect tense, since we have the imperfect of the auxiliary verb. The addition of the final 'e' is a point many candidates will forget, even if they write the remainder of the phrase correctly, but you should make it a rule that whenever you have written a preceding direct object pronoun you check whether a past participle agreement is required.

(6) Here you should have no problem if you think sensibly. Avoid the temptation to assume 'comme on t . . .' which the foolhardy might easily do. (You should in any case recognise that 'comm*ent*' and 'comme *on*' involve different sounds, but the world of O-level is not a perfect one.)

(10) Make a mental note that the speaker is feminine, therefore a past participle agreement is called for.

(14) Two dangers lurk here: if you recognise the first you should avoid the second. Again it is largely a question of what you expect to follow grammatically from the preceding phrase – the first half of the idiom 'to have the time to do . . .=avoir le temps/*de faire* . . .' Therefore the first syllable heard cannot constitute the first complete syllable of a weird French word ('degs . . .') but must be 'd' + ex . . .'.

This should lead you automatically to complete the word with the infinitive ending '–er'. Should you still be 'dans le brouillard' by the time the following phrase is dictated, you should have the gumption to redeem yourself when you hear clearly an obviously parallel phrase 'de+verb in infinitive'. But perhaps that is an optimistic viewpoint.

(16) There will be many who vainly try to make up some form of a plural noun along the lines 'les critures', but – common sense to the rescue again! – think of the context, (letters, envelopes, etc.). The maid recognises Mademoiselle's . . . ? 'Writing' should not be an impossibly difficult idea and once on that track the possibility of a singular noun should occur.

(30) Seen in written form the noun would present no problem, but in a dictation the situation will be very different. Apply the procedure of checking possible spellings from the sound heard '–an, –en, –am, –em') and see what emerges.

In addition to these major areas of possible difficulty, this dictation, as every other, contains words so commonplace as to be scarcely worth mentioning (you may think,) but which will undoubtedly be mis-spelt by hundreds of candidates. These are: **heureuse; l'adresse; mademoiselle; connaissez; monsieur; brouillard.** If *you* mis-spell these, learn them thoroughly *now*!

In the third and final section of this exercise you have five minutes in which to correct your completed version. The passage will be read through again fairly slowly, as on the first reading, and this will be your last opportunity to check the sound of the passage as a whole. Try to keep a special ear open for endings of adjectives and nouns. Have a pencil ready to make light underlinings of words or phrases you will need to think about particularly during your checking time. What you must *not* do is to concentrate on these there and then, or you will miss what follows.

In the allotted five minutes you must go through your version, systematically checking every phrase. Check that:
1. it makes **sense** (if not, consider alternative spellings or word combinations which could make sense);
2. **every clause** has a **main verb** with an ending you can justify;
3. **every other verb dependent** on that main verb is in the infinitive;
4. **every verb agrees** with its **subject, every adjective** with its **noun,** both in gender and number;
5. there is **consistency** between **article** and **adjective** (e.g. la petite, or le petit, but not a mixture of the two);
6. **accents** are **consistent** and **clear;**

7. you have left **no ambiguities** or **alternatives** and that what you have written is **legible**;
8. you have **not consciously written** anything which you know to be **wrong**, and you have **not ignored sound and sense** to create your private version (e.g. producing 'ma montre' when you heard 'm'a montré').

If you can satisfy yourself on all above counts then you have probably done the best you can.

Student answer

Tous les vendredis, à onze heures précisément, Madame Mercier quittait son appartement pour aller faire ses courses de la fin de semaine. Ce matin-là, elle a mis son meilleur manteau et son plus joli chapeau et elle est descendue en bas, portant au bras son sac à provisions. Après avoir salué d'un sourire la concierge qui balayait la cour, elle est partie pour le marché. Elle est entrée d'abord chez le boucher, où elle a choisi deux belles côtelettes d'agneau. Puis elle s'est dirigée vers l'épicerie. En y entrant, elle s'est rendu compte avec plaisir qu'il y avait devant la comptoir quelques-unes de ses voisines qui bavardaient avec le boutiquier.
'Bonjour, tout le monde,' a-t-elle crié d'une voix gaie. 'Vous connaissez la nouvelle? Mon fils vient de se fiancer. Vous serez tous invités au mariage cet été.'

(The Associated Examining Board)

Student answer

(1) Tou*t* les vendred*i*, (2) à onze heures précis*e*ment, (3) Madame Mercier quittait son appartement pour aller faire ses cour*s* de la fin de semaine. (4) Ce *matin là*, elle a mis son meilleur manteau et son plus joli chapeau, et elle est descendue en bas, portant au bras son sac à provisions. (5) Après avoir salu*er* d'*en* sourire (6) la concierge qui ba*l*ayait la cour, elle est partie pour le marché. Elle est entrée d'abord chez le boucher, (7) où elle a choisi deux belles *cutlettes danyo*. Puis elle s'est dirigée vers l'épicerie. (8) *En entrant*, elle s'est rend*ue conte* avec plaisir qu'il y avait devant le *comtoir* quelques-*uns* de ses voisines, (9) qui bavard*ait* avec le boutiquier.
'Bonjour, tout le monde,' a-t-elle crié, (10) d'*un* voix *gai*. 'Vous connaissez la nouvelle? (11) Mon fils vient de *sa* fianc*ée*. (12) Vous serez tous invit*er* au ma*rr*iage *cette* été'.

Comments With twenty full points lost this is an average offering. But most of these errors are due to carelessness which a thorough knowledge of relevant grammatical structures would have prevented. Occasionally the candidate has refused to accept the sounds he has heard and has invented alternative versions either to suit a pre-conceived idea he has formed, or to fit in with the English spelling of an equivalent word.

(1) Consequential or repeated errors are not normally penalised a second time: here, however, I have the distinct impression the candidate was not even thinking of an ending for either word, far less making them agree with each other.

(2) The omission of the accent has occurred because the candidate has not concentrated hard enough. He has heard the first 'é' and should have recognised exactly the same sound in this syllable.

(3) Of course the phrase (=to go shopping) should be a familiar one at this level, but in any case the final 's' sound heard has been totally misrepresented.

(4) Presumably the candidate knows this use of the demonstrative adjective, but has carelessly omitted the hyphen.

(5) A careless error – how can the infinitive ending be justified? *d'en* . . .: In the first place the two sounds (the original and this one) are quite different, and in the second, no sense can be made from the phrase as it stands here. The candidate should have realised this and made a pencil note to listen closely to that phrase on the final reading, in the hope of producing the correct solution.

(6) Simply a spelling error, but the word should be known.

(7) *d'agneau* has obviously caused great heart searching: at least there is an attempt at correct phonetic rendering! The spelling of the preceding word is very remiss; since the word obviously means 'cutlets', the candidate has decided apparently that it must be spelt more or less as in English, despite a clear 'o' sound and enunciation of three separate syllables.

(8) Presumably because he was unable to see the function of the pronoun 'y', the candidate has decided not to hear it! You must write down *all* you hear. One can commiserate with the past participle error but alas! this is one instance where the reflexive pronoun is **indirect** object ('rendered account **to herself**') and therefore the participle does not agree.

conte is phonetically accurate but incorrect. One would have expected the candidate to be familiar with the expression.

comtoir: this is a frequent mis-spelling of a very common word.

uns: First the candidate has ignored the evidence of his ears ('uns' and 'unes' are not close enough in sound to be confused), and secondly he has fallen down on the rule of checking that consistency is maintained. He should have spotted the discrepancy between pronoun and noun (voisi*nes*).

(9) This is a bad error and should have been eliminated when the candidate was checking verb/subject agreements.

(10) This is an example of an error which should never have occurred. 'Voix' is a common noun, and the gender should be known, apart from the fact that, as we have just seen above, the sounds involved in the error are not alike.

(11) Here we see how the candidate has altered what he has heard to suit his own idea of how the phrase should read. He dismissed the fact that the sound was 's*e*', happy in the thought that the substitute version seems to fit in well with the general meaning.

(12) What justification is there for an infinitive ending? This is the future tense of the passive.

marriage: a common mis-spelling.

cette été: At O-level the candidate would be expected to know both that 'été' is a masculine noun and also that the form of the demonstrative adjective before a masculine noun beginning with a vowel is 'cet'. But then one expects many things which do not seem to materialise!

Common errors

Candidates are often anxious about the dictation and make the mistake of putting pen to paper immediately the exam supervisor begins each phrase. This means that concentration is divided between listening to the second half of the phrase while trying to write the first half. Force yourself to **listen hard to the whole phrase, then write.**

Too many candidates **spend too long over a word** or phrase they cannot understand. Leave a blank space and go back to it later. (You may then be able to make sense of it by considering it in its context.) In any case if you are not ready to concentrate on the following phrase you are likely to make a mess of that as well.

Legibility and accuracy are of prime importance; you must ensure that your style of writing contains no weird idiosyncracies unintelligible to others, and that it is neat. **On no account** should you try to hedge all bets by offering **alternatives** or by writing letters or accents which could be variously interpreted.

They will be interpreted as wrong.

In spite of the fact that candidates must surely know all punctuation is given in French, a surprising number still try to incorporate 'virgule' or 'à la ligne' into their answer. **You must learn the punctuation indications.**

Concerning lexical errors, we have seen earlier how a large proportion revolve round **verb forms.** These should be the principal focus of your attention during the checking period, as outlined earlier in the chapter.

Difficulties in **recognising word boundaries**, especially where groups of words involve liaison or elision ('qu'ils ont', 'l'a mis'), lead to many errors. Get into the habit of mentally computing all spelling possibilities for the sounds you hear ('l'ami(e)', 'la mi– . . .'; 'la manger', 'l'a mangé(e)', etc.) There will only be one alternative which fits into the surrounding grammatical structure.

Phonetic errors account for very many mistakes, of course. By O-level you should know the basic rules of pronunciation and although there may be some problem in differentiating 'ais/é' sounds, your knowledge of grammar, together with the context, ought to supply the correct solution, even if your ear cannot. The 'é' and 'è' sounds are quite different from each other, as are the single and double 's' sounds (cf. 'plaisait' and 'connaissait'), but confusion between these occurs often nevertheless. Apart from these mistakes concerning general principles we have seen how many marks are lost through the **mis-spelling of the most everyday words**, which candidates have simply never bothered to learn properly.

Last but by no means least is the question of the dictation making **sense.** Writing phrases which make no sense is a cardinal sin!

Translation into English

This is an exercise which candidates often feel they can tackle with confidence because they are producing their own language in the answer. However, this confidence may lead to careless rendering of the original French – not enough attention to detail, for instance. The dangers which spring from an over-confident approach will be examined more closely a little later in the chapter.

Model answers

A. *Martine et Viola éclatèrent de rire, car grand-père venait de laisser tomber un haricot dans son verre à vin. Félix prit le plat des mains de Martine et le passa à maman, qui se servit. Puis, voyant que l'assiette de Félix était toujours vide, elle lui rendit le plat. Ils étaient si nombreux que, quand tout le monde fut servi, grand-mère avait déjà fini.*

Papa s'aperçut que personne ne buvait; il remplit donc les verres, un à un, puis il demanda à sa femme, d'un ton inquiet:

– Ma chérie, c'est tout ce qu'il y a pour le dîner?

– Mais non. J'ai pensé que le jambon serait meilleur avec la salade. Va le chercher, Viola.

Viola ne bougea pas.

– Viola, tu entends? Tu n'es pas sourde, non?

– Mais non, maman.

– Alors, fais ce que je te dis, veux-tu ... et pendant que tu es là, tu pourras apporter encore du vin rouge. Ton père en voudra avec le fromage.

Viola sortit enfin, pas du tout contente. Autrefois, quand ils habitaient cette grande maison à Paris, ils avaient des domestiques pour accomplir ces tâches, et les membres de la famille pouvaient rester assis à table pendant que Jeannine, la bonne, enlevait les assiettes vides et portait les plats de la cuisine. Maintenant tout était changé. Maman était obligée de faire elle-même la cuisine, tandis que Viola et Martine devaient faire toutes sortes de choses désagréables. Elles avaient même à faire la vaisselle!

(The Associated Examining Board)

Model answer

Martine and Viola burst out laughing, for Grandfather had just dropped a bean in his wine glass. Félix took the serving dish from

Martine and handed it to Mother, who helped herself. Then, seeing that Felix's plate was still empty, she gave the dish back to him. There were so many of them at table that by time every one was served grandmother had already finished. Father noticed that no one was drinking, so he filled up the glasses one at a time, then anxiously asked his wife:

– Darling, is that all there is for dinner?

– Of course not. I thought that the ham would go better with the salad. Go and fetch it, Viola.

Viola did not move.

– Viola, do you hear what I say? You're not deaf, I suppose?

– No, Mother.

– Well then, do as I tell you, will you . . . and while you're about it you can bring in some more red wine. Your father will be wanting some with the cheese.

Viola finally left the room, not at all pleased. Previously when they lived in the big house in Paris there were servants to carry out these tasks and the members of the family could remain seated at table while Jeannine the maid took away the empty plates and brought in the serving dishes from the kitchen. Now everything was different. Mother was forced to do the cooking herself, while Viola and Martine had all sorts of unpleasant jobs to do. They even had to do the washing up!

B.   *A vision of the moon*

Les 384 000 kilomètres furent vite franchis. Cela ne prit plus de temps que le trajet Paris–New York dans les vieux avions supersoniques. La fusée se posa sans la moindre difficulté sur le sol poussiéreux.

– Eh bien, nous voici, dit le major Weissli. – Soldats, continua-t-il, à cette minute votre nom entre dans l'immortalité. Vous avez fait de la Lune la banlieue de la Terre.

– C'est moins joli que la baie de Naples, dit le soldat Cuttolo.

– Il paraît qu'il fait plus de cinquante degrés au-dessous de zéro, ajouta le soldat Pamonski. Pire que Leningrad au mois de février.

L'expédition passa une semaine sur la Lune et fit un grand nombre de photographies. Après quoi, elle remonta dans la fusée et revint sur la Terre où on l'accueillit avec des cris de joie admiratifs. Le major Weissli avait aussi rapporté beaucoup d'échantillons minéraux que les laboratoires analysèrent passionnément.

Un mois s'écoula, puis deux mois, puis un an, puis deux ans. On envoya encore quelque fusées dans la Lune malgré la petite fortune que cela coûtait chaque fois. Hélas, il devenait de plus en plus évident que l'on ne pouvait rien faire avec cette planète. Impossible d'y semer la moindre plante ou d'en faire un centre de tourisme.

On créa un Comité International pour lequel on construisit un magnifique bâtiment à Genève. Au bout de cinq années de travaux assidus, on décida de bâtir sur la Lune un immense cinéma de 30 000 places où l'on passerait de beaux films montrant la vie sur la Terre!

(Southern Universities Joint Board)

Model answer

The 384,000 kilometres were rapidly covered. It took no longer than the journey from Paris to New York in the old supersonic planes. The rocket landed without the slightest difficulty on the dusty ground.

– Well, here we are, said Major Weissli. – Soldiers, he went on; at this very moment your name is going down in history. You've made the Moon the Earth's suburb.

– It's not as beautiful as the Bay of Naples, said Private Cuttolo.

– Apparently the temperature gets down to 50 degrees below zero, added Private Pamonski. Worse than Leningrad in February.

The expedition spent a week on the Moon and took a considerable number of photographs. After this the men climbed back into the rocket and returned to Earth to be welcomed with joyful cries of admiration. Major Weissli had also brought back with him a lot of mineral samples which were eagerly analysed in the laboratories. A month went by, then two, then a year, then two years. A few more rockets were sent to the Moon, in spite of the small fortune it cost each time. But unfortunately it was becoming more and more obvious that nothing could be done with this planet. It was impossible to sow even the tiniest plant or to develop it as a tourist centre.

An International Committee was set up and a magnificent building was constructed for it in Geneva. After five years' hard work it was decided there should be built on the Moon an enormous cinema to hold 30,000 people, where splendid films would be shown depicting life on Earth!

Answer plan

It is absolutely essential to read the passage through at least once before beginning to think of a translation. You should then read it through more carefully a second time, noting by underlining in pencil the words or phrases you are unfamiliar with or which you anticipate will cause some difficulty. There is really no need at all to begin writing within the first five minutes or so:

it is far better to use thinking time at the start, trying to obtain a grasp of the overall meaning of the passage and identifying the difficulties, than to rush to set pen to paper and then find yourself with fifteen or more minutes at the end of the examination with little to do but twiddle your thumbs. Let us therefore apply this approach to the following passage:

(1) *Dans leur cellule improvisée, Michel et Daniel comprirent qu'ils ne pouvaient pas espérer se libérer seuls. Les cordes qui liaient leurs bras étaient trop bien attachées.*

(2) *Le plus ennuyeux, dit Michel, c'est que nous nous sommes conduits comme des bébés! J'aurais mieux fait d'entrer le premier et toi, tu serais resté dehors. Tu aurais pu alerter l'oncle François!*

(3) *Il y avait longtemps déjà qu'ils étaient allongés sur le sol de leur prison lorsqu'ils crurent entendre approcher quelqu'un. En même temps des rayons de lumière filtrèrent à travers les planches mal jointes de la porte.*

(4) *– Qu'est-ce que ... ? commença Michel.*
Mais le bruit d'une clef dans la serrure l'interrompit. – Daniel, chuchota-t-il, ne dis rien! On va essayer de faire tomber celui-là s'il est seul!

(5) *Ils retinrent leur respiration de sorte que les moindres mouvements de l'arrivant étaient perceptibles. Mais le nouveau venu ne pénétra pas dans la grotte. Il se contenta d'appeler, sans trop élever la voix:*
– Monsieur Michel? Monsieur Daniel? ... Vous êtes là? Tout étonnés, les jeunes gens mirent quelques secondes à deviner qui pouvait les appeler ainsi.

(University of Cambridge Local Examinations Syndicate)

From a first reading you will have understood that the passage relates an incident written in the past (main tense past historic), in which two boys have been tied up and locked in a makeshift prison. They are wondering how they might free themselves. The words 'les cordes', 'liaient', 'attachées', 'le bruit d'une clef', and of course 'prison' should have indicated this to you, even if the words 'la cellule' and 'la serrure' were not known. This meagre knowledge should predispose you to making, where necessary, some sensible guesses. Secondly you should look for any difficulties or unknown words. A possible list here might be:
le plus ennuyant: a superlative, but what does it refer to?
nous nous sommes conduits: what is the meaning when reflexive?
j'aurais mieux fait de: exact tense rendering is difficult,
tu aurais pu: here the difficulties are increased!

ils retinrent leur respiration: which verb is this taken from?

celui-là: this needs careful translation in English.

de sorte que: this may not be known and an intelligent guess may be required.

mirent . . . à deviner: what is the purpose of 'mettre' here?

Now you should begin your rough draft. In translation from French there are two basic requirements, **accuracy and good English**. You must achieve a version which takes full account of all the nuances of the French, but which at the same time does not sound stilted and unnatural in English. On your first draft accuracy must be the primary consideration.

(1) In the first sentence you will be able to follow the word order of the original without alteration. You should note that *pouvaient* is in the imperfect tense, but by checking mentally the reason for this (description of the boys' state of mind), you should realise that you will only need to provide a simple past tense in translation, ('could not hope to . . .'). Any other translation normally associated with the imperfect tense is patently not suitable here. Similarly in the following sentence the verb *liaient* is in the imperfect tense because it **describes** their state. Therefore 'which tied' is correct.

(2) Here you will have to think sensibly. *Le plus ennuyeux,* a superlative without a noun, and which continues *c'est que . . .* must obviously be referring to a situation or an idea, and in fact represents the way of expressing in French 'the most . . . *thing* (about it/them, etc.) is . . .' In your English translation, therefore, you must supply the idea which is implied in French: you must say 'the most annoying thing about it is that . . .' Remember translation requirement no. 2 – **write good English.**

Next comes the question of the verb *conduire* used reflexively. You should know that this means 'to behave, to act'. At the end of the same phrase (*comme des bébés*) you should calculate that this is clearly an occasion where translation of the article would not be correct. You must say 'acted like babies'.

The remainder of this section offers difficulties only in tense – *aurais fait, serais resté, aurais pu+infinitive* are all conditional perfect tense='would have done'. The use of *pouvoir* in the last example poses some additional difficulty in this tense because of the particular meanings possible with this verb. 'Could have . . ., might have been able to . . .' especially must be mastered.

The translation of this section should therefore be: 'It would

35

have been better for me to go in first and you would have stayed outside. You could have warned Uncle François.' Here are two further points:

toi, tu . . .: this represents emphasis, as we might achieve in English by underlining the written word or by stressing the spoken word. Neither device is permissible in French. It would of course be totally un-English to be slavishly literal and write 'you, you.' A candidate silly enough to try this would be penalised on two counts, poor style and lack of common sense.

l'oncle François: titles in French require the definite article but this is not English usage and so you must omit it in translation.

(3) *il y a (avait)* + *time expression* + *que and clause* should be a familiar structure to the O-level candidate. The meaning is: 'X has (had) been doing . . . for X length of time.' It is a structure which should be as familiar as the parallel one *depuis* + *verb* (present or imperfect). Failure to recognise this will certainly lead to nonsensical English, and to begin 'there was . . .' just because this is often a correct version of that phrase in isolation spells immediate disaster. **Look at the whole phrase** before translating any part of it. In this case, then, the sense is: 'They had already been lying on the ground?/floor? of their prison for a long time when . . .' Again in this sentence there are two or three things to point out which are going to make the difference between an adequate and a good translation.

(a) the position of *déjà*: find its natural place in English. This will *not* be 'a long time already'.

(b) the exact shade of meaning of *allongés*: there are several words in French to indicate lying down (*couché* = 'lying', i.e. not sitting; *étendu* = 'stretched out'; *allongé* = 'lying', showing merely that you are on a horizontal plane!) An O-level candidate should, of course, be fully aware that it is the French *past participle* which renders the English present participle ('-ing') in these cases.

(c) *le sol* = 'ground, earth', indicating that their prison has a natural floor. But the normal phrase needed here would be 'floor'.

ils crurent entendre approcher quelqu'un: this is a phrase which well illustrates the difference between English and French usage. The French contains a whole string of infinitives which must *not* be translated literally in English. What seems to fit best? – 'they thought they could hear someone approaching.'

(4) *on va essayer*: the translation of *on* always requires thought. Is it 'they, we, people, someone' – the most usual meanings? Here of course you must choose 'we', and you must go on to

36

express the natural meaning in the context of *on va + infin*. Expressing future intention you must select 'we will try . . .' *not* 'we are going to try.'

celui-là: this can, of course, mean 'the former' or 'that one', (when choosing between alternatives). Neither makes good sense here, however, so you should ask yourself what *is* its purpose. Surely it is to give emphasis – 'the fellow out there'.

(5) *ils retinrent leur respiration*: this is the past historic of the irregular verb *retenir* = 'to hold back'. Is the 'back' necessary in English? If not, leave it out.

les moindres: the comparative or (here) superlative form of *petit* and often it carries the meaning 'slightest' as an alternative to 'least'.

perceptibles: beware using a direct equivalent just because one exists in English. Might not 'could be heard' prove a better translation here?

de sorte que: candidates may know that this conjunction has two meanings; followed by the indicative mood (as here), it means 'with the result that . . .'; followed by the subjunctive mood it means 'in order that . . .'. You will need to be very precise to avoid error.

sans trop élever la voix: yet again the difference in use of the article between the two languages is illustrated. In English you must say 'without raising his voice too much.'

mirent + time à infinitive: as with an earlier phrase the use of *mettre* in this way should be a structure familiar to candidates. It means 'to take (time) to do . . .'.

qui pouvait les appeler: once more the question of tense is important here, with the same conclusion applying as in a previous instance. A simple 'could' suffices, giving the final phrase 'who could be calling them in this way'.

If you as a candidate had tackled this translation in the manner recommended here, minutely examining each nuance of meaning, you could be satisfied that your rendering contained no inaccuracies or gross distortions of English.

Finally you should read through what you have written in order to polish up your English, **without reference to the French text**. If you do decide to alter anything at this stage, then check back to the French to make sure you have not strayed too far from the original shade of meaning.

37

Looking for somewhere to live

C'est juste à ce moment que l'étranger entra. Il était grand, mince, et paraissait âgé de vingt-huit à trente ans. Il portait un sac sur l'épaule. Il vint au comptoir.

– Il n'est pas trop tard pour avoir un café ? demanda-t-il.

– Je veux bien vous servir, dit Mathilde. Pourtant, d'habitude, tous les soirs à cette heure-ci, je ferme . . . sauf le samedi et le dimanche. Elle posa devant lui une tasse de café fumant, avança le sucrier. Il prit deux sucres, remua le liquide, et le but presque brûlant. Les autres le regardaient en silence. Il se tourna vers eux :

– Je cherche une chambre à louer. Vous n'en connaissez pas une ?

– Non, répondit Hippolyte. Il ajouta en se levant, mais sans regarder l'étranger : Demandez à la patronne ; elle en loue, des chambres.

– J'en ai deux, mais elles sont prises, dit Mathilde. Mais vous pouvez aller voir chez Madame Martin.

Gabriel lui sourit, et suggéra :

– C'est sur notre chemin. Viens, on te conduira.

L'argent de l'inconnu claqua sur le comptoir. Il était prêt à sortir quand la porte s'ouvrit, et un petit garçon d'environ sept ans pénétra dans la café, accompagné d'un immense chien, entièrement blanc.

– J'avais peur que ce soit fermé, alors je me dépêchais ! . . . Je viens chercher du tabac pour César.

Il alla vers le comptoir, suivi de sa bête, et tous lui firent place à cause d'elle. L'étranger avança la main, il allait la poser sur la tête du chien, mais le chien gronda, et il la retira tout de suite.

(Associated Examination Board)

Student answer

It is just at this moment that the stranger entered. He was *big*, thin and *seemed aged from 28 to 30* years. He carried a bag *on the shoulder*. He came to the counter.

– It is not too late to have a coffee? he asked.

– I *will serve you well*, said Mathilde. However *as usual every evening, I will be closing at this hour* . . . except Saturdays and Sundays. She put before him a *steaming cup of coffee* and pushed across a *saucer*. He took two sugar lumps, *tasted* the liquid and drank it almost *burning*. The others were looking at him in silence. He turned *round* to them:

– I am looking for a *bedroom to hire*. You don't know *one of them?*

– No, replied Hippolyte. He ———— while getting up,

but without looking at the stranger; Ask the *patron*; she hires rooms, *some of them*.
– I have *two of them*, but they are taken, said Mathilde. But you can *go to see* at Madame Martin's house.
Gabriel smiled, and suggested:
– It's on our way. Come, *someone will lead you*.
The money of the man dropped on to the counter. *He was nearly going out* when the door *opened itself*, and a little boy, *of almost seven years penetrated into* the cafe, accompanied by *an immense dog, entirely white*.
– I was afraid that it *should* be shut, therefore I was hurrying! . . . I *am coming to look for* the tobacco for César.
He went towards the counter, followed by his animal, and all made a place *for her*. The stranger put out his hand, he was going to put it on the dog's head, but the dog *groaned* and *it retained* the hand at once.

Comments On the whole this is not a bad answer although, as you will see, it could have been so much better with relatively little effort and common sense and by following the guidelines laid down in the previous section. Apart from the errors, there is something about the translation which suggests it has not been written by someone whose native tongue is English, and even supposing there were no actual errors, it is this fault which would prevent the translation earning really high marks.

it is just: common sense should have encouraged the candidate to adapt the French present tense to the more natural-sounding 'it was just . . .'

big: the candidate should have said 'tall', since height is almost always the dimension implied when *grand* refers to people.

and seemed . . . years: this does not sound natural. Look away from the French and think of the idea itself. Then you might well find the expression 'seemed about 28 to 30 years old'.

on the shoulder: as in the previous section, we notice the use of definite articles. You must say 'on his shoulder'.

I will serve you well: this is a mis-translation. For this to be correct we should have seen '*Je vous servirai bien*'. The phrase concerned here is *vouloir bien*='to do something willingly', giving the idea 'I'll gladly serve you'.

as usual . . . this hour: 'as usual=comme d'habitude.' The one word 'usually' therefore changes the sense of the verb and gives, correctly, 'However usually I close at this time every evening'.

a steaming cup of coffee: a petty difference you may think, but the adjective *fumant* (masc. sing.) must describe the coffee.

pushed across a saucer: 'pushed across' is a good suggestion for *avança*, but *le sucrier* is 'sugar basin'. For two reasons the candidate should have known better: first the mention of *sucre* in the following line should have encouraged an intelligent guess. Numerous near-analogies should have helped too: une pomme= an apple, un pommier=an apple tree: du café=coffee, une cafetière=a coffee pot. Secondly the candidate should have known the word for saucer=*la soucoupe* and should therefore not have written down something he knew to be wrong.

tasted the liquid: a possible correct guess but in fact *remuer*= 'to move', hence here 'to stir'.

burning: this is a word-for-word translation; a more appropriate translation would be 'scalding, boiling hot'.

he turned round to them: unfortunately for this candidate he has confused two similar phrases *se tourner vers*='to turn towards' (but not necessarily right round) and *se retourner*='to turn right round'. This is an easy error but a trap commonly set by examiners.

a bedroom to hire: two points need mentioning here, both interconnected. 'A room' is sufficiently precise to render *une chambre* in this context, which makes it apparent by the addition of *à louer*='to rent'. In English he would obviously be wanting to sleep there, whereas in French this is only apparent if the word *chambre* is used. This is one of those instances where the French are very particular to use the word which conveys the exact meaning; the alternatives *une pièce, une salle* would not be correct.

you don't know one of them: – *she hires some of them*: – *I have two of them*: these three phrases involve the same point, namely the use of the object pronoun *en*. To recap, *en* is necessary in French whenever a number or quantity is indicated of a noun understood but not stated. *En* replaces that noun in the sentence but can nearly always be omitted in the English version, with subsequent improvement to the sound of the sentence.

Compare these improved suggestions with the candidate's original: *you don't know of one? She has rooms to rent. I have two.*

he —————— *while getting up*: you should *never* leave blanks, you *must* suggest something. The verb *ajouter* should be known, of course; it occurs frequently in translation passages and means 'to add'. *While doing* . . . is not always a very natural way of expressing the simultaneous action implied in French. Try 'as he

40

stood up' – or simply omit the 'while'.

ask the patron: a false friend! More often than not a word which clearly has an identical form to a French one is misleading. This is, of course, not the correct use of the word in English and the candidate should have been wary enough not to follow that particular red herring!

you can go to see: this is an example of 'the lure of the French' proving a positive hindrance to good English. We always say 'go and do', but the candidate has obviously been attracted to the infinitive form of the French. Incidentally, in the same sentence it would be wise to leave out the word 'house'. The apostrophe of possession (Madame Martin's) is usually quite enough to indicate house or premises as the case may be.

Gabriel smiled: the candidate has (by design?) omitted the word *lui*. It is the indirect object pronoun referring to a person, and so must be rendered 'smiled at him'.

someone will lead you: no! not 'someone'! As well as being totally generalised, *on* refers to the recognised subject of the sentence (we, they, you) and here, according to common sense, this must be *we*. Thus 'we will show you the way'.

The money . . . the counter: first, you would normally say 'the man's money'. Secondly, the candidate should be well aware that 'dropped', were it correct, would have involved the verb *tomber*. *Claquer* is in fact an onomatopoeic word meaning 'to slam' (doors, etc.).

he was nearly going out: this is a bad mis-reading; the candidate imagines he has seen *près de*= 'near to'. What he should have said is 'was ready to go out'.

the door opened itself: very clever stuff! The reflexive verb is used, you will remember, in accordance with normal practice, *but* it is unnecessary in translation. *Ouvrir* is a verb which may have an object; in cases where it does not, then a reflexive form of the verb is required.

a little boy of almost . . . the café: as in the first sentence, natural phraseology has been disregarded. There is also a mistake, *environ*= 'approximately' has been mistaken for *presque*= 'almost'. The ending of this sentence also sounds rather odd. This is not an occasion for using the nearest English equivalent to fit *pénétra*. The idea is obvious, so the candidate should exert himself a little to produce something more acceptable, like 'a little boy aged about seven came right into the café'.

by an immense dog, entirely white: each word here is undoubtedly correct, *but* it could have been expressed better, for instance 'accompanied by a huge dog, white from head to tail'.

afraid . . . should be shut: the subjunctive! An instant case for panic in the eyes of many! Forget its terrors; in translation render it just as sounds most natural, 'afraid that it would be shut'. Only a few tenses of the subjunctive remain in regular use and so you will obviously find yourself having to manipulate this mood in translation.

I am coming to look for: a case for common sense. The candidate should realise that he can profitably and without qualm adjust the tense of *je viens* to read 'I have come'. To his shame he has also manifested a common failing; he has not recognised *chercher* as 'to fetch', or 'to collect'.

and all made a place for her: here is an example of the brain registering a word or two correctly and then inventing the rest of the phrase to fit, regardless of the evidence. This almost never pays off, and if it appears to be a recurring tendency it is a sure way to irritate the examiner. The phrase should read 'everyone made room for him on account of it'. (You must avoid the temptation to write 'of her', since *elle* refers of course to the feminine noun *la bête*.)

the dog groaned: common sense again would have prevented this error. *Gronder*='to scold', and here 'to growl'. Dogs do that!

and it . . . at once: in theory *il* could well refer to the last mentioned masculine noun, but here it does not. It should be apparent that we are referring to the stranger.

retirer:='to pull back' (literally). The best conclusion to the passage would therefore be 'and he drew back his hand at once'.

From these corrections it should be possible to see how a moderately acceptable answer can quite readily be transformed into an answer of merit.

Common errors

Notorious 'black spots' for weaker candidates are the **inability to handle tenses correctly** and **pronoun problems**. Since you must translate the passage, you cannot choose to avoid dealing with these areas, as you could perhaps do elsewhere by writing in one tense only and omitting pronouns.

Tenses, therefore, represent the biggest source of error in this examination. Weaknesses and lack of confidence will show themselves by failure to recognise tenses correctly, resulting (in translation from French) in the wrong meaning being attached to certain phrases. This can often also have repercussions throughout a whole passage, as the candidate, having made one bad error, continues to make consequential errors to fit in with the original. The first essential, therefore, is to recognise and render each tense accurately. A group of verbs which highlight this necessity particularly are the modal verbs (pouvoir, devoir, etc.), which are normally used with another verb. Examples of these have been seen in the sample questions examined earlier.

Pronouns spring up all over the place. You cannot ignore them if you dislike or mistrust them because they will be there for you to deal with. They make bad enemies so it is advisable to decide you will be master. Not only will you need to know the straightforward uses of all pronouns, but, as we have seen only recently in the chapter, you will need to be able to handle idiomatic uses of pronouns.

Poor quality English is a further major area where candidates not only lose, but actually squander marks. By now it should be quite clear how important is good written English style. Candidates erring in this respect usually fall into one of three main categories. First there are those who translate word for word, with no thought of creating a passage of readable prose. Secondly there are those who adopt too colloquial a tone (one accompanied all too often by a goodly sprinkling of spelling mistakes and even actual faults of grammar). Many translation papers bear the warning words 'Mistakes in grammar and spelling will be penalised' – they do mean this! The third category are those who fail to differentiate between various types of registers of language. You will probably have noticed that many passages contain some narrative and also some conversation. It is important to demonstrate in your translation that (just as in real life) different tones of language will be appropriate to narrative on the one hand and conversation on the other. A special problem is posed by such common French turns of phrase as *on . . .*, *il faut . . .* and other impersonal constructions. This very important point is emphasised in a final note on the last page of this chapter.

Alternatives and blank spaces. It is simply a waste of time and space (not to mention the examiner's good humour) to adopt either of these strategies. In the first the candidate hopes to hedge his bet, imagining for some unaccountable reason that the examiner will himself make the right choice between two or more options. You cannot sit on the fence – *you* must decide. If you do not, you will find the examiner simply ignores all alternatives (including any correct one), and you will therefore gain nothing at all. Similarly, if you leave blank sections you are actually harming your chances – what is not there cannot be given credit. If you guess sensibly you stand at least some chance of finding the right word or phrase, even if it is only by accident. Too many candidates are defeatist and frankly do not put enough effort into trying to sort out difficulties. Obviously you are not meant to be familiar with every single turn of phrase or item of vocabulary – there would be little or no test if this were the case. You are, in part, being tested on your ability to make intelligent deductions from the information before you. Clues for difficult sections may be found in the general or specific context (the whole passage or merely the previous or following sentences), in parts of words you may recognise (e.g. *lent* = 'slow', ra*lent*ir = 'to slow down') or indeed in the use of the same unknown word or group of words in a slightly different context elsewhere. In short, a candidate with a healthy ration of common sense can earn himself considerable credit, which has not a great deal to do with innate linguistic ability.

Haste and blindness. The latter fault may sound severe but is very common. In a way it is the reverse of the preceding point. Here we are thinking of the candidate who knows that what he is writing is wrong because not everything fits together, but chooses to ignore the fact, presumably in an effort to have something to set down on paper! In this situation you must work from the elements you know to be right and build up possibilities from there. Allied with this fault is the too hasty approach. The candidate *thinks* he has seen a certain phrase, or he sees half a phrase and invents the remainder! This is not the key to success!

Just as a sobering post-script, the 1976 Examiners' Report from one major Board reminds the candidates that they will be penalised just as much for omitting e.g. '*puis*', as for being unable to translate '*embouteillage*'. It is fairly widespread practice for many candidates to ignore words of this kind (*donc, d'ailleurs, pourtant, déjà* are other examples) – at their peril! Finally, do *not* translate '*on . . .*' as 'one . . .'; '*il faut*' as 'it is necessary'; or '*n'est-ce pas?*' as 'is it not?'. Nearly always it will be **totally inappropriate** and you may well lose marks for poor English style. It is necessary, therefore, for one to find alternatives, is it not? You see what I mean?

Translation into French

Model answers

A. *My father and sister leave the house every morning at eight o'clock. I don't leave until a quarter to nine and then mother is alone with her dog and cat! This morning she said to me: 'Wait for me, Paul. I am coming with you as I want to do the shopping early. Tomorrow is your grandmother's birthday and we must send her a card. As a present, father and I have decided to buy a new armchair for her. We saw one last week in a shop window and I want to look at it again.' 'Are we going to see Grandmother tomorrow?' I asked. 'Of course. As it is Saturday, father is going to fetch her in the car and she will spend the day with us here.'*

(Southern Universities Joint Board)

Model answer

Mon père et ma soeur quittent la maison tous les matins à huit heures. Je ne pars qu'à neuf heures moins le quart et ma mère se trouve alors toute seule avec son chien et son chat! Ce matin elle m'a dit: 'Attends-moi Paul. Je viens avec toi comme je veux faire les courses de bonne heure. Demain c'est l'anniversaire de ta grand'mère et il nous faut lui envoyer une carte. Comme cadeau ton père et moi nous avons décidé de lui acheter un fauteuil neuf. Nous en avons vu un la semaine dernière à la vitrine d'un magasin et je veux le regarder encore une fois.' 'Est-ce que nous allons voir grand'mère demain?' ai-je demandé. 'Naturellement. Comme c'est samedi, papa va la chercher dans la voiture et elle passera la journée avec nous ici.'

B. *Mr and Mrs Thomas, Michael and Ann were spending the holidays at the seaside. One day the sun was not shining and the weather was cold.*
'What are we going to do today?' said Mr Thomas after breakfast.
'Let's go to Mapelton as it is too cold for the sea,' replied his wife. 'There are many interesting places to see there and it is only thirty miles from here. We can visit the castle, the big market and there are some fine shops.'
'I don't want to see any shops,' cried Michael.
'No, but you and father can walk round the town while Ann and I do some shopping.'
'A very good idea,' said Mr Thomas. 'Michael doesn't like shops,

but he can come with me to the garage. I want to look at some new tyres and then we can go to the chemist's as I need some films for my camera.

(Southern Universities Joint Board)

Model answer

Monsieur et Madame Thomas, Michel et Anne passaient les vacances au bord de la mer. Un jour le soleil ne brillait pas et il faisait froid.

'Qu'allons-nous faire aujourd'hui?' a dit Monsieur Thomas après le petit déjeuner.

'Allons à Mapleton comme il fait trop froid pour la mer,' a répondu sa femme. 'Il y a là beaucoup d'endroits intéressants à voir et il ne se trouve qu'à quarante-cinq kilomètres d'ici. On pourra visiter le château, le grand marché et il y a de beaux magasins.'

'Je ne veux pas voir de magasins', s'est écrié Michel.

'Non, mais papa et toi vous pourrez faire une promenade en ville pendant qu'Anne et moi nous ferons des achats.'

'Quelle bonne idée', a dit Monsieur Thomas. 'Michel n'aime pas les magasins, mais il pourra venir avec moi au garage. Je veux regarder de nouveaux pneus et puis nous pourrons aller chez le pharmacien, comme j'ai besoin de pellicules pour mon appareil de photo.'

Answer plan

Translation into French is an exacting exercise, a collection of vocabulary and idioms taken from those you should have studied during your course, and formed into a story of sorts. You must **never** see each word as a single unit to be translated in isolation – it fits into a surrounding phrase and must be considered in the context of the whole phrase. The passage is certain to be written in the past. Your teacher will have instructed you as to which of the two main narrative tenses you will be required to use (past historic or perfect), and **you must stick to this instruction**. Remember, of course, that there will be a place for other tenses to be used in conjunction with the main tense (here assumed to be the perfect). As always you should first read the whole passage. Now try your rough draft, taking a section at a time. With your pencil underline real difficulties in the manner indicated in the previous chapter. Whatever you do, you should not, either at this point or later, spend a disproportionate amount of time brooding on bits you do not know: get on with what you do know and consider problems afterwards.

(1) *Last year we invited grandma to come and spend a weekend with us. She lives alone in a small flat. She never watches television and she does not go out much.*

(2) *After three days we were all irritated, and even the dog looked ill. I must explain that grandma talks all the time, but does not allow us to reply.*

(3) *She is not one of those charming old ladies who adore children. On the contrary, she detests them. The first day she told John that his hair was too long.*

(4) *The next morning she asked Jane why students were so lazy and why they demonstrated in the streets. 'We didn't do that when I was young,' she said.*

(5) *On Sunday evening she astonished my parents by saying: 'Your children don't resemble you at all. Where did they learn their terrible manners?' I shall go abroad before her next visit.*

(to demonstrate=manifester)

(Oxford and Cambridge Schools Examination Board)

(1) Here you should have no difficulty identifying *invited* as perfect tense (=nouns avons invité). and the remaining verbs, *lives* (=habite), *watches* (=regarde+direct object), *does not go out* (=ne sort pas) as straightforward present tenses. You will not, of course, be tempted to introduce any auxiliary form with the last verb . . . enough said!

'L'année dernière' is a phrase very much on the list of prescribed O-level learning, as are all other similar expressions (next week, last year, etc.).

Dependent on the verb *invite* is *to come*, and dependent on that is *and spend*. Recognition of the idioms and structures which have been laid out ready to trap the unwary is important in this exercise, so you should **consciously register each point**, as with the two examples here. By so doing you will have remembered:

(a) *inviter* requires *à* before the following infinitive, and

(b) *aller* requires a direct infinitive to follow.

with is worthy of a moment's reflection. Is it really 'avec', or does it mean 'at our house=chez'? You decide.

Adjectives in this section offer no problem, a feminine agreement for *alone* (=seule) and masculine for *small*, and the word order of the paragraph is also straightforward.

(2) In this section you will not find a single perfect tense; the two past tenses are clearly imperfect since they describe people's state

of mind (=nous étions, avait l'air). The remaining ones are again present, *must* (=je dois), *talks* (=parle), *does not allow* (=ne nous permet pas . . .). There are several verbs to be found in a dictionary under the heading 'to look'. It is to be hoped you know which is which, and would certainly not have been foolish enough to write 'regarder'. If you do not know why, find out at once. If you could not remember 'avoir l'air', but knew 'regarder' was wrong, then 'sembler=to seem' would have made an acceptable alternative.

In this section we have two dependent verbs (both therefore will be in the infinitive form), *explain* and *reply*. How they are governed (direct infinitive, or the prepositions 'à' or 'de') must be a matter you consider before writing anything; you should of course register '*je dois expliquer*' and '*. . . permet (pas) de répondre*'. The indirect object of 'permettre' is here rendered by the pronoun 'nous'.

irritated and *even* could (but should not) pose problems. 'Irrité' exists and even if you did not know 'même', you could try a substitute ('et le chien aussi'), which, while being considerably less than excellent, is at least more desirable than a blank space. **Always remember a blank space cannot possibly gain you any marks** whereas a substitute just might earn you something. The various forms of 'tout' (adjective and pronoun) are generally known rather badly by candidates: here, of course, you need the masculine plural adjective (=tous irrités), and for *all the time* the uncomplicated form 'tout le temps'.

(3) There is one perfect tense called for here, *she told* (=elle a dit) and one imperfect, *his hair was* . . . Otherwise there are further present tenses. The candidate who, in spite of advice, persists in translating each word as it comes along will be in trouble with the last phrase – if not before, of course! But the candidate who follows advice and considers the phrase as a whole should recognise the difference in English and French idiom where personal descriptions are concerned. He should remember the French 'avoir les cheveux longs', should recall that he had already decided the required tense was the imperfect (=il avait) and should then easily be able to adapt the remainder of the phrase (=les cheveux trop longs).

The candidate's awareness of the French version of *told X that . . .* should help him with 'permettre à X de+infinitive', since the same question of an **indirect object** applies.

on the contrary (=au contraire) is an item of vocabulary you can be expected to know well.

In the first sentence we have two adjectives describing the same noun (*charming old ladies*). Adjectives need to be considered in two ways, first the agreement and second the position. In this case, both adjectives must be feminine plural: as for position, 'old' is a before-the-noun adjective, whereas 'charming' is not.

This gives the following: 'une de ces vieilles dames charmantes'. Incidentally both 'vieux' and 'cheveux' figure on any list of the ten most mis-spelt words, so be warned!

At the end of the first sentence what you will need to add in French to express the generalisation contained in the phrase *adore children* is of course the definite article.

There is only one pronoun here, *detests them*, for which the position will be the regular one before the verb.

(4) Here the two verbs *she asked* (=elle a demandé) and *she said* are the ones in the perfect. You will be aware that the second occurs after direct speech and therefore inversion will be necessary (=a-t-elle dit). If you have any difficulty recognising all other verbs as imperfect you will need to check this point very carefully. The construction with 'demander' is precisely the same as that with 'dire' (indirect object) and so you will need the preposition 'à' before the noun.

the next morning is a phrase to be expected (=le lendemain matin) and you should be able to cope with it as a matter of course.

that is a word which candidates often mis-manage. It all depends on which 'that' it is! It can be a conjunction (='que', joining two clauses), a relative pronoun (='qui', 'que', etc.), a demonstrative adjective (='ce', 'cette', etc.) or a neuter pronoun (='cela'). Clearly the latter is the correct form here; *that* refers to 'the student demonstrations'.

(5) The perfect tense main verbs are *she astonished* (=elle a étonné), *did they learn?* (=ont-ils appris?). *Resemble* is present tense, and *I shall go* is obviously future.

by saying is a verbal construction which you should know how to render as a present participle (=en disant).

Time expressions of various kinds are constantly being tested in all papers of the examination. *On Sunday evening* is a typical example and you should be well aware that *no* preposition is required in French. 'Dimanche soir' correctly conveys the phrase.

resemble offers two potential sources of error. There will be candidates who forget to double the 's' in French, and there will be others (or quite possibly the same ones) who forget the need – yet again – for an indirect object (=ressembler à quelqu'un). In this case slight protection may be afforded by the fact that the object is the pronoun 'vous'.

at all should not cause difficulty if you remember it is really part of the negative form 'pas du tout'.

In spite of the emphasis in this passage on verb constructions, candidates have been treated fairly leniently as regards the verbs themselves, with few irregular forms being tested. In this last section we have two (the past participle of the verb 'apprendre' and the future tense of the verb 'aller') The accompanying phrase in the last example (=à l'étranger) should be well-known, but if by chance you could not recall it, you should be sensible enough to offer an alternative (perhaps 'dans un autre pays').

terrible manners may indeed necessitate more than a moment's thought. Some candidates may not know 'des manières', although it is really common enough and a great many will jauntily write 'des terribles manières', even assuming the noun to be correctly resurrected from the recesses of the mind. This innocuous-looking phrase is in fact one of the ones which will sort out the first-rate candidate from the rest, because he will (a) beware of using 'terrible', remembering 'affreux' instead; (b) remember to make a feminine plural agreement, and (c) place it correctly to give 'leurs manières affreuses'.

In the final phrase all self-respecting O-level hopefuls will hit upon the right word for *before* in a time sense and will carefully calculate the position of *next* in view of the fact it is qualified by *her* and has the meaning of 'following'. In other words – 'avant sa prochaine visite'.

Having come to the end of your rough draft (taking about forty minutes) you should then **check through** the piece carefully, giving some concentrated attention to any section you are unhappy with or had omitted earlier. Use the check list below (under point 6) to make sure you have covered all foreseeable sources of error. When making your fair copy ensure that you **copy clearly and correctly, leaving nothing out**. If you have time, it is wise to check your fair copy minutely phrase by phrase against the exam question.

In résumé, then, here is a recommended list of procedures to help you do your best on this exercise.
1. **Read through the whole passage.**
2. **Isolate particular problem phrases.**
3. **Decide on the tenses** of the verbs within each section.
4. Consciously **register the difficulties** being tested, especially where differences of idiom are concerned.
5. **Never translate one word without fitting it into its**

context, adjusting it as the need arises.

6. Carry out the following **systematic grammatical check;**
   (a) **every main verb agrees with its subject**, and carries the correct ending for the tense selected;
   (b) **every dependent verb is in the infinitive**, and preceded by 'à' or 'de', if this is required by the verb on which it depends;
   (c) **every main past tense remains consistently perfect or past historic;**
   (d) **every necessary past participle agreement is made** (be especially careful in cases of preceding direct objects);
   (e) **every adjective agrees** with its noun or pronoun;
   (f) **every pronoun is correct in gender and number;**
   (g) **object pronouns are correctly positioned** in relation to the function of the verb;
   (h) **adjectives and adverbs are correctly positioned;**
   (i) **tu/vous forms** (with their corresponding adjective or pronoun forms) remain **consistent;**
   (j) **spelling** (including accents) is careful and clearly written.
7. **Read your finished version through very thoroughly.**

Student answer

'I'm going to the bank,' Michael said. 'Suzanne, you can prepare the picnic and don't forget the fruit juice.' He left, but returned after a quarter of an hour and they were soon ready to set off.
'We ought to hurry,' said Suzanne. 'The others are waiting for us. We are supposed to be outside the cinema before half-past eleven – we must not be late.' 'We have enough time,' replied Michael. 'They won't be there on time.'
Finally they set off on their mopeds without their friends. In the afternoon, tired because it was beginning to get very hot, they stopped to rest a little. They quickly went to sleep. When they woke up Michael called to his sister. 'Look! Someone has stolen our mopeds.' 'What can we do?' wondered Suzanne. 'We are a long way from home.'

Student answer

'Je vais à la banque' *Michel a dit.* 'Suzanne, tu peux préparer le pique-nique et *tu doit n'oublies pas* le jus de fruits.' Il est parti, mais *a retourné* après un quart d'heure et ils étaient bientôt *prêts de se mettre.*
'*Nous devons se dépêcher*' a dit Suzanne; 'Les autres nous

attendent. Nous devons être devant le cinéma avant onze heures et demie – *nous ne devons pas en retard.*' 'Nous avons *assez temps*' a répondu Michel. 'Ils ne seront pas là *à temps.*'

Enfin ils *se sont mis sur leurs vélomoteurs* sans leurs amis. L'après-midi, fatigués parce qu'*il commencait d'être très chaud*, ils se sont arrêtés se reposer un peu. *Ils ont vite dormi.* Quand ils se sont réveillés, Michel *a appelé à* sa soeur. 'Regarde! Quelqu'un a volé nos vélomoteurs.'

'Que faire?' *a demandé Suzanne.* 'Nous sommes loin de chez nous.'

Comments This version displays several typical (and often puzzling) features of a script. Although the candidate tackles the whole thing well, some mistakes are surprising – but examiners find this is the case each year.

Michel a dit: candidates often forget to invert the verb after direct speech. In the other instances where a similar phrase occurs in the passage the candidate has written correctly *a dit Suzanne*, etc., doubtless helped by the English presentation.

tu doit n'oublies pas: this is an awful mess! and has probably arisen because the phrase was not viewed as a whole. The candidate should have applied the usual rule: identify the tense of the verb (=command form), ignore totally the English 'don't' – all it does is show that this command is a negative, decide the ending (='tu' form), remind himself that '-er' verbs lose the final 's' in the second person singular command form, and hey presto! – '*n'oublie pas*'!

a retourné: 'retourner' is a verb conjugated with 'être', giving *est retourné*e (or *est rentré*, as an equally acceptable alternative).

prêts de se mettre: just as you must learn the verbs which require a preposition before a following verb, so also must you know thoroughly those adjectives which require 'à' or 'de' to follow them. Here we have the wrong one: in addition the candidate has only half remembered the phrase 'to set off'. The whole phrase should read – *prêts à se mettre en route*.

nous devons se dépêcher: the examiners seem keen on testing the verb 'devoir' in a variety of tenses in this passage. They do present some difficulty and should be thoroughly mastered. 'Ought' is in fact the conditional tense; we should therefore see here *nous devrions* followed, of course, by a compatible reflexive pronoun before the infinitive. Thus *nous devrions nous dépêcher*. It is pleasing to see that the candidate has coped with the two other examples of 'devoir'. You should particularly note one of the possible meanings of the present tense (=we are supposed to).

en retard: one of those surprising features! You would have expected a candidate who was familiar with the phrase to realise that 'être' was the necessary first element (=*être en retard*).

assez temps: all these expressions of quantity (beaucoup, trop, tant, etc.) are followed by 'de' before the item mentioned. This is rather an elementary mistake.

se mettre sur leurs vélomoteurs: since the omission of 'en route' is a repetition of a previous error, the candidate will not be penalised a second time. *Sur leurs vélomoteurs* is likely to be a very 'popular' error, but candidates will reasonably be expected to be able to produce *en vélomoteur*. After all they have probably had 'means of transport' on their language agenda for at least four years by the time O-level is reached. **The ability to apply what you know in a different context** is a measure of likely success in this examination.

il commencait d'être très chaud: there are three errors here:

(a) the candidate has forgotten the 'ç' necessary in certain tenses and persons of verbs ending in '–cer'.

(b) it is impossible that at this level the candidate has not seen, heard and personally used many times the verb 'commencer' with a following infinitive preceded by the preposition '*à*'.

(c) as previously the candidate has not applied what he un- doubtedly knows in theory, namely that weather expressions use the verb 'faire'. The correct phrase is: *commençait à faire très chaud*.

a appelé à sa soeur: the idiomatic use of prepositions is a tricky area in any language, but certain verbs ('chercher', 'regarder', 'attendre', etc.) are so frequently encountered from the earliest stages of learning French that the candidate should be able to handle them automatically at this level. 'Appeler' is a similar verb, followed by the direct object only, i.e. no preposition.

a demandé: how strange that a candidate who has handled a testing idiom like *que faire* confidently should not also know the verb 'to wonder=se demander'. By making this error he has of course avoided what was intended as the real challenge here, namely the question of the past participle agreement. *S'est demandé Suzanne* is correct because the reflexive pronoun, being indirect object, will attract no agreement.

Common errors

The prose (translation into French) aims to test manipulation of common idioms and items of everyday vocabulary in a simple context. The candidate should not need to resort to guesswork, much less to the ludicrous Inspector Clouzot style of fractured French which unfortunately occurs all too often. 'Elle a tookè offé ses spectacles' will appeal in no way to an examiner. The language of the prose is always limited to the linguistic experience which can reasonably be expected after five years' study. The candidate does not need, however, to **make a real effort to analyse the passage in terms of that experience.** You are not faced with the unknown (or should not be): somewhere and probably many times previously you have met and practised the structures and vocabulary contained in the passage for translation. But failure to recognise these structures and idioms, **failure to view phrases as a whole,** and to eliminate word-for-word translation, without reference to the total phrase, will surely spell disaster. As we have seen, even when candidates are familiar with the separate components of any given phrase, they come to grief by their inability to fit them together correctly; in other words they are unable to cope with the syntax of the language. In practice this usually means that the candidate has thought to a certain degree, but has not carried out the thinking process to its conclusion. Here is a further example: *My father had just left the old man when* ... The (average) half-processed thinking will register the two main points (the idiom 'to have just—venir de'; 'old' is an adjective which precedes the noun), ponder no further and will probably come up with something like: *Mon pére vient de quitter le vieux homme quand* ... which, quite frankly, is no better than total ignorance. The next process should have been to decide which of the two tenses associated with the idiom is correct in this instance, and to note that since the masculine form of the adjective occurs before a noun beginning with a mute 'h', the special form *'vieil'* will be needed (or alternatively the noun *'le vieillard'*). It does seem a pity that the relatively small effort required to carry the thought process through to the right conclusion is not made by candidates. It really is worth it. Candidates who have developed almost as a reflex action the grammatical checking procedure outlined on pages 50–1 will of course be less prone to making such syntactical errors.

Inconsistency of the **main past tense** is very common, as is the **misuse of the imperfect tense** in conjunction with this. In virtually all cases tense usage is clear cut and with practice you should not have difficulty in making these kinds of decisions. Confusion between other tenses, together with the **inability to**

recognise and differentiate the compound tenses (pluper-fect, etc.) is also common. Constructions involving following infinitives present many difficulties, it seems, as do **the participles** (past and present).

Pronouns, in whatever form, seem to wreak havoc. As regards object pronouns, the three possible positions (when object of a main verb, of an infinitive, or of a command) are not well enough known in practice by most candidates. Distinction between object and emphatic pronouns is often blurred, and few candidates seem happy to use demonstrative and possessive pronouns, much less any but the most basic of relative pronouns.

Question forms, question words and negative expressions are also areas where many flounder and yet in no respect can these elements be termed advanced. In fact they are fundamental.

Confusion between verbs which share one English meaning (e.g. 'laisser', 'quitter', 'partir'=to leave) still catch out many candidates, although one must assume the differences are well stressed during the O-level course. On similar lines, there are perennial problems with such words as 'pleuvoir'/'pleurer'; 'argent'/'monnaie'/'agent'; 'raconter'/'rencontrer'; 'dire'/'parler', and many others.

We have seen many illustrations of the potential black-spots presented by **agreements of all kinds**. Maybe 'black-out' would describe the situation more accurately.

Lastly, to complete any remaining gaps in a picture of gloom, mention must be made of the **paucity of vocab** witnessed in very many scripts. Common words and idioms which litter the pages of any French text or grammar book are not known, and the inevitable conclusion must be that they have never been really learnt. The same criticism is true of **genders** which, for even the most basic of nouns, appear not only totally haphazardly selected, but are also inconsistent (e.g. la/le maison; le/la fille).

The final homily must record that the weak, the feeble-minded and the lazy will inevitably find here their just deserts. On the other hand the conscientious candidate who has made a good effort over the preceding five years and is prepared to be careful and thoughtful at the time of the exam should find that he can tackle this exercise (and all others) with a good degree of success.

Comprehension

Under this heading many different exercises are included for which the skills being tested will differ considerably. There are four possibilities:

(a) written test with questions to be answered in English;
(b) written test with questions to be answered in French;
(c) aural test with questions to be answered in English;
(d) aural test with either questions to be answered in French or reproduction in French of the story read aloud.

Sometimes multiple choice answers are the formula, and you should not be fooled into thinking this is a soft option. Only *one* answer of the alternatives is wholly satisfactory – there will be at least one feature about the others which will eliminate them. With only one correct answer there is no leeway for partial credit.

Where original answers are required in French the word 'comprehension' does not adequately cover the situation being tested, since it is the candidate's ability to manipulate elements of the language which is in question. The demands made on the candidate, when written reproduction of a story presented aurally is the test, are similar and equally taxing. An aural test cannot usefully be simulated in this form and will therefore be dealt with fairly briefly in the planning section of the chapter.

Model answers

A. *Read carefully the following passage. Then, without translating it, answer* **in French** *the questions following it.* (*The past historic tense, e.g.* il donna, *should not be used in your answers.*)

A worrying experience

Jérôme Espardon est garagiste au village d'Ecoin, à cinq kilomètres de Nevers, sur la grand' route de Paris. Il y a un mois à peu près, le premier octobre, ayant toujours du travail à faire, il décida de se coucher plus tard que d'habitude. A onze heures, pendant qu'il se trouvait dans le petit bureau qui était au fond du garage, un bruit lui fit lever la tête. Une voiture venait de s'arrêter, et peu de temps après, on frappa à la porte. D'abord, il ne voulut pas l'ouvrir:
– Généralement, me dit-il plus tard, je refuse de servir les clients la nuit, de peur d'être attaqué, ce qui est arrivé à un de mes amis . . . et

puis j'ai toujours beaucoup d'argent dans le bureau: je ne voudrais pas le perdre.

Mais, étant toujours habillé, il ouvrit la petite porte. Un homme était là, mais dans l'obscurité Espardon ne put distinguer son visage.

– Trente litres d'essence, dit-il, et faites vite!

Pendant qu'il manoeuvrait la pompe, Espardon regarda bien la voiture. Il se souvint plus tard du numéro de la voiture: 26 RV 06 . . . 'Alpes-Maritimes, c'est bien loin, ça,' pensait-il. Et puis deux personnes, un homme et une femme, étaient assises sur la banquette arrière.

Le client lui remit un billet de cinquante francs, en lui disant de garder la monnaie. Au moment où il reprenait sa place dans la voiture et où il mettait le moteur en marche, la vitre arrière commença à s'ouvrir, et, au grand étonnement du garagiste, la main d'une femme apparut et une voix cria 'Au secours! Aidez-moi!' C'était une voix de femme, mais elle se perdit tout de suite dans le bruit de l'auto, qui accéléra bien vite et partit à toute vitesse dans la direction de Paris.

– En rentrant, dit Espardon plus tard, je me suis dit: 'Préviens donc la police', mais je me suis tout de suite rappelé: 'Voilà quatre jours que le téléphone est en panne.' J'étais seul au garage, ma femme étant encore en vacances chez ses parents, en Savoie; il n'y avait personne avec qui discuter de cet incident bizarre. 'C'est peut-être une plaisanterie,' ai-je pensé, et j'ai décidé que je ne devrais pas y attacher beaucoup d'importance.

Mais une fois couché, il se trouva incapable de dormir, à cause de ces paroles pleines de terreur, et, vers cinq heures du matin, il se présenta à la gendarmerie la plus proche où il fit une déclaration, que tous les journaux reproduisirent, et qui causa bien des conversations animées dans le voisinage. La gendarmerie, cependant, se contenta de téléphoner à Nevers pour savoir si, cette nuit-là, il y avait eu dans la région quelque événement anormal. Mais on n'avait signalé aucun accident, aucune alerte. D'ailleurs un gendarme avait été en faction sur la route toute la nuit, à l'entrée de la petite ville de Pouilly, à deux kilomètres de là, et il avait noté le numéro de toutes les voitures qui passaient, mais – pas de 26 RV 06. L'inspecteur eut même l'audace de lui dire:

– Vous ne l'avez pas rêvé, monsieur?

1. Le premier octobre, quelle décision Espardon a-t-il prise, et pourquoi?
2. Quels bruits a-t-il entendus pendant qu'il travaillait?
3. Pourquoi n'a-t-il pas voulu ouvrir la porte d'abord?

4. *Pourquoi n'a-t-il pas pu voir le visage du client?*
5. *Qu'est-ce qui indique que le client était pressé?*
6. *En manoeuvrant la pompe, qu'est-ce qu'Espardon a remarqué?*
7. *Pourquoi le garagiste était-il étonné?*
8. *Pourquoi n'a-t-il pas pu aider la femme?*
9. *Qu'est-ce qu'il avait l'intention de faire en rentrant, et pourquoi ne l'a-t-il pas fait?*
10. *Qu'est-ce qui l'a empêché de dormir?*
11. *Quelles indications y a-t-il que la police ne l'a pas pris très au sérieux?*

(The Associated Examining Board)

Model answer

1. Il a décidé de se coucher plus tard que d'habitude ce jour-là, parce qu'il n'avait pas encore fini son travail.
2. Il a entendu le bruit d'une voiture qui s'arrêtait, et aussi le bruit d'un coup à la porte.
3. Parce qu'il avait peur d'être attaqué, et il ne voulait pas risquer de perdre l'argent dans son bureau.
4. Parce que dehors il faisait noir.
5. Le client a demandé à Espardon de se dépêcher en faisant le plein d'essence.
6. Il a remarqué le numéro d'immatriculation de la voiture.
7. Parce que la dame assise sur la banquette arrière a ouvert la vitre et a crié à l'aide.
8. Parce que la voiture a accéléré tout d'un coup et est partie très rapidement.
9. Il avait l'intention de prévenir la police mais il ne l'a pas fait car son téléphone était en panne.
10. Le souvenir des paroles de la femme dans la voiture l'a empêché de dormir.
11. La police n'a fait que téléphoner à une autre gendarmerie pour savoir si l'on avait vu la voiture, et puis l'inspecteur a demandé à Espardon s'il n'avait pas inventé l'histoire.

B. *Do not translate the following passage, but read it carefully before answering the questions:*

Tout à coup Philippe aperçut un prêtre qui se dirigeait vers le quai. Et quelques instants après il vit une seconde forme sortir de l'ombre. Le drame ne dura pas plus d'un instant. Il n'y eut pas de cri, pas d'appel. Seulement le bruit d'une chute dans l'eau. L'homme qui avait suivi le prêtre se jeta sur lui, le précipita dans le bassin et aussitôt s'élança du côté de la ville. Après un premier moment de surprise Philippe se débarassa de ses souliers et il se jeta du haut du parapet pour porter secours à la victime, qui, assommée par cette attaque, devait se noyer sans même avoir repris connaissance. Au bout de quelques instants il réussit à le saisir par ses vêtements, et, lui maintenant la tête hors de l'eau, il regagna le mur du quai, nageant d'un bras. Il se leva, traînant son fardeau jusqu'au pavé où il le déposa avec précaution. Au bout de quelques minutes d'exercices respiratoires, de mouvements de bras que lui avait appris son oncle, Philippe eut la grande joie d'entendre le premier cri du blessé. Il respirait maintenant et Philippe écrasait sous ses genoux son ventre pour lui faire rendre à pleine gorgée l'eau boueuse dont il était rempli. Bientôt le prêtre ouvrit les yeux et prononça quelques mots. D'abord, sans doute, son nom que Philippe ne comprit pas, puis un numéro et d'autres mots: 28, rue du Chasseur . . . son adresse? Epuisé par cet effort, l'homme avait perdu à nouveau connaissance. Philippe, sans penser qu'on pouvait être inquiet de lui, chargea alors le noyé sur ses épaules et se mit en route vers l'adresse où l'homme avait sa maison. En chemin, après plusieurs haltes pour se reposer, il trouva enfin le numéro 28; une belle villa avec un grand jardin. Il y avait de la lumière à l'intérieur. Philippe frappa plusieurs fois et enfin une vieille gouvernante vint ouvrir.

Answer by brief sentences in English, confining your answers to the material provided by the passage set.
1. What did the second man do to the priest?
2. How did Philippe bring the priest back to land?
3. Why did Philippe need to take further action to help the priest after hearing the latter's first words?
4. What two pieces of information did he gather that these words were trying to convey?
5. What are we told about the way the priest was taken home?

(Southern Universities Joint Board)

Model answer
1. He leapt upon the priest and pushed him in the water.
2. He grabbed the man's clothes, and, holding his head above water with one arm, used the other to swim to the quayside.
3. Because the priest had lost consciousness again.
4. Philippe gathered that the words referred to the man's name and address.
5. Philippe carried the priest over his shoulders.

Answer plan

In this section the type of exercise illustrated in the first Model Answer is chosen, with brief comments on the other major exercises which feature under the title of 'comprehension.'

Passage with answers in French

The need for a thorough first reading of the passage should be quite obvious here – you must have a clear idea of the essential points of the story before you attempt to answer any questions.

A fine Sunday afternoon in and around Toulouse

Jeanne et Pierre s'étaient installés pour déjeuner à la terrasse du restaurant. Dans la rue, les familles se promenaient sous un ciel bleu.

– Vous ne mangez donc pas chez vous aujourd'hui? demanda Jeanne.

– Non, ma mère est en visite chez une cousine, répondit Pierre. Et vous?

– Mes parents ne m'attendent pas avant le soir. Ils iront probablement au cinéma comme tous les dimanches.

Sur le trottoir d'en face, venant de la gare, un groupe d'hommes, coiffés de bonnets de papier aux couleurs rouge et or, s'avançait en criant 'Allez, Perpignan!'

– Regardez, voilà les supporters qui arrivent! En effet, j'avais oublié le fameux match de rugby! Vous allez au stade?

– Ah non, malheureusement je n'ai pas de place. Je vais faire un petit tour à la campagne, voir mon ami Daniel Legrand qui habite à Saint-Julien.

– Excellente idée, approuva Jeanne. On pourrait aller tous les deux dans ma Renault. D'accord? Alors, je compte sur vous pour m'indiquer la route. Allons!

Les deux amis se trouvaient bientôt en pleine campagne. Sur les petites places des villages, les villageois jouaient aux boules et les vieilles gens prenaient le soleil en les regardant. La Renault roulait depuis une demi-heure quand Pierre s'exclama:

– Ralentissez! Là, là, prenez sur la gauche . . . n'oubliez pas votre clignotant, s'il vous plaît! Attention à cette Citroën sur vos talons, qui veut vous doubler.

Jeanne vira à gauche sur un chemin tranquille qui descendait doucement au village. Elle franchit un pont, suivit une rue et déboucha sur la place. Elle s'arrêta. Tout était calme; deux ou trois vieilles femmes se dirigeaient vers l'église; trois voitures de tourisme stationnaient devant le café – leurs occupants s'attardaient évidemment sur le repas de midi. Face à la Mairie se trouvait le *bazar, tenu par Daniel Legrand et sa femme. Pierre poussa la porte, faisant tinter une petite clochette, et ils pénétrèrent dans une salle encombrée; l'on apercevait un comptoir surchargé d'**illustrés,** de journaux, de boîtes d'articles de pêche. Derrière le comptoir, des piles d'espadrilles et de pantoufles, quelques instruments de jardinage . . . une impression de désordre où l'on pourrait trouver n'importe quoi.*

– Oui oui, j'arrive, cria une voix. Un bruit d'assiettes parvint de l'arrière-boutique, et une femme se montra.

– C'est pour quoi?

– Bonjour Madame, dit Pierre, Daniel serait-il là?

*– Ah non, je regrette. Il est à Toulouse pour le match. Ils sont partis tout un groupe, en **car**, ce matin. Un match de cette importance, vous savez!*

Answer **in French** *the following questions.*
Each answer should be concise but should include all relevant information and must suit the tense of the question.
Full marks will not be awarded for phrases or sentences directly copied from the text.

1. *Qu'est-ce qui vous indique qu'il fait beau temps à Toulouse? Donnez **deux** indications.*
2. *Comment est-ce que les supporters de Perpignan indiquent quelle est leur équipe préférée?*
3. *Comment savez-vous que Jeanne ne connait pas la route à Saint-Julien?*
4. *Vous êtes Jeanne. Ecrivez ce que vous avez fait pour vous rendre au village ('Jeanne vira . . . Elle s'arréta'). Commencez 'J'ai viré . . .'*
5. *A quoi sert un clignotant sur une voiture?*
6. *Qu'est-ce qui vous fait penser qu'il y a une rivière à Saint-Julien?*
7. *Que faisait Madame Legrand quand Jeanne et Pierre sont arrivés?*
8. *Comment savait-elle qu'on avait ouvert la porte du bazar?*
9. *Exprimez autrement en français: '**illustrés car**'; (above).*
10. *D'après ce texte, donnez **deux** façons de passer l'après-midi en ville, et **deux** façons de le passer à la campagne. Commencez chaque phrase par 'on' (Exemple: 'on se promène dans la rue').*

(Oxford and Cambridge Schools Examination Board)

This passage demonstrates that you cannot always expect a nicely rounded story with a neat ending. The text is descriptive and contains no dramatic events, although its focus is an important rugby match. From your first reading you should gather that the culmination of the story is indeed a total anti-climax. Now you should read carefully through all the questions. You will notice the very useful advice given in the instructions printed just before the questions. All points made there are ones on which candidates fall down year after year, and you would do well to heed what is printed there. As you are examining the questions, glance back to locate the section which contains the factual information for each answer, remembering that the questions always follow the order of the passage. As on previous occasions you may find it profitable to underline in pencil relevant phrases. The following may sound an unnecessary statement of the obvious but experience of examiners has proved otherwise – you must know *precisely* what is being asked in each question. Normally a variety of question forms will be used and by the time you sit the exam you should be well acquainted with the way each needs to be tackled. If you are not, then you are not prepared for the exam, and should remedy the situation right away.

Let us take the forms presented here one by one:
1. **Qu'est-ce qui indique que . . .?** (=what indicates that . . .?) You may answer in one of two ways:
   (a) 'Ce qui l'indique, c'est que . . .+relevant facts';
   (b) (much more simply) state the facts as they stand.
   The first suggestion is more polished and used correctly would be sure to find favour with the examiner.
2. **Comment est-ce que . . .?** (=in what way . . .?) The neatest way of answering this question is by means of a present participle – 'en . . .-ant'.
3. **Comment savez-vous que . . .?** (=how do you know that . . .?) Here a present participle would be incorrect. You should say 'Je le sais parce que . . .
4. In this question you are required to transpose the text from 3rd to 1st person singular.
5. **A quoi sert . . .?** (=What is . . . used for?) A straightforward reply is called for here, '. . . sert à+infinitive'.
6. **Qu'est-ce qui vous fait penser que . . .?** (=what makes you think that . . .?). As in question 1, there are two main alternatives:
   (a) 'C'est que+clause giving relevant facts';
   (b) again simply state the facts.
7. **Que faisait . . .?** (=what was . . . doing?) Reply simply by

62

giving the necessary details in the imperfect tense.

8. **Comment savait-elle que . . .?** (=how did she know that . . .?) This is a repeat formula of question 3, with tense and person altered.

9. **Exprimez autrement** (=express in other words): a recommended turn of phrase here would be: 'A la place de . . . on pourrait écrire . . .'

10. Here you are simply required to make four statements as indicated in the example.

It should never be forgotten that this exercise is an exacting one. Nevertheless there are still candidates who believe that all they have to do is copy sections of the text as they stand. (*Please* take note of the instructions.) Even if a particular section could provide a grammatically correct answer, full credit is not given for such minimal effort. Almost invariably there will be a more commonplace turn of phrase which you could be expected to know, and which conveys the same idea – and this is what is meant by *using French*. More often than not, however, it is necessary to reconstruct the text to provide answers which are grammatically correct and which answer the question asked. You should be particularly aware of the way in which this reconstruction will necessitate your **adjusting tenses, changing the persons of the verb, pronouns, switching from direct to indirect speech or v.v., turning infinitive constructions into finite tenses** and so on. There is a great deal to consider.

Now to examine closely the requirements of the questions here in terms of grammatical structure.

1. Assuming throughout that facts are not going to pose any problems, your first check must be the **tense of the question**. Decide how this will affect your own answer, since it is very often the case that the tense of the question and answer will be the same. Then consider how you may **express the ideas** (here two are asked for) **in your own words** ('manger dehors', 'prendre le déjeuner à la terrasse'; 'faire des promenades au soleil', 'faire beau' are good and simple expressions).

2. Because a present participle is to be used, the question of tense does not apply here. To complete your participle phrase, which would logically be based on the verb 'porter', by repetition of the phrase 'des bonnets de papier . . . rouge et or' could not be expected to earn a pat on the back, whereas a simpler invention of your own could well do so. At least it would show that you have tried.

3. The information within the text for this answer occurs in a passage of direct speech, and so will require considerable manipulation to produce a correct answer. You will certainly need to think out the way of using in French the construction 'to ask someone to do', and you will need to use this in the perfect tense. You will also need to think hard about which object pronoun will be correct if you are restructuring the phrase 'm'indiquer la route' as indirect speech.

4. Here you have to transpose tenses and subjects. The correct tense is indicated in the question – perfect tense – and even if the verbs 'franchir', 'déboucher' were not known, the past historic endings in the text show they are perfectly regular of their type.

5. The first element of this question is, of course, a test of vocabulary. It is perfectly reasonable to expect this word to be known at O-level, but inevitably there will be candidates who will not know and will have to guess. If you examine the context sensibly it should be possible to do this successfully. A suggested definition might be 'indiquer la direction que va prendre la voiture.'

6. The tense you will require in the clause following 'C'est que . . .' is, of course, once more the perfect. A synonym of the verb 'franchir' would be 'traverser', a verb surely known to O-level candidates. No special problems are involved in using this verb in your answer, and, as previously, its use would show that you had thought sensibly about the question asked.

7. You must deduce what Madame Legrand was doing from the phrase given ('un bruit d'assiettes . . . boutique'). The imperfect tense has already been indicated in the question and the phrase needed to complete a satisfactory answer is plainly 'faire la vaisselle'. A simple alternative to 'arrière-boutique' would also be advisable – this can be easily done by a relative clause describing the position of the room.

8. Whether you choose to present the information from the point of view of Madame Legrand (what she had heard) or from that of the visitors (that they had made the shop bell ring) is immaterial, *provided* that you respect the need for the pluperfect tense.

9. Candidates should not experience real difficulty in finding substitute vocabulary items for the ones in bold type ('des revues', 'des magazines', and 'un autobus').

10. This seems a relatively simple question, with every possible indication given in the question form to help the candidate. Nevertheless there are many who cannot accurately express

themselves in the present tense in the examination.

In any one test of this nature you will of course meet only a selection of possible question forms; you must therefore be totally prepared for all of these.

Passage with answers in English

This is a different exercise altogether from the one examined above. The level and extent of your comprehension of French is being investigated, and not your ability to express yourself in the foreign language. The passage, therefore, is likely to be of a correspondingly higher linguistic standard, and it is probable that there will be more emphasis on the meaning of precise words or phrases.

Assuming that you are able to overcome difficulties of this nature you must then ensure that the information you give in your answers is **relevant, gives all the details asked for, but no more, and is written in good English**. As in the translation of French into English you will be penalised for poor English grammar, spelling or punctuation. Repetition of information or unnecessary detail will waste time and serve no useful purpose. Since, you will remember, the questions follow the order of events in the passage, and there is no overlap between questions, careful reading of the questions before beginning to write should prevent this kind of error.

Passage with multiple choice answers

Once more you must proceed along the same lines at the outset. By taking time to come to terms with the sense of the passage (or the situational dialogues) and by reading it thoroughly, you will be able to make a more reasoned decision when it comes to examining the nuances of each possible answer. For this is what the exercise is all about. There is not necessarily one alternative which stands out immediately as the right answer. This may depend on the **correct interpretation of one word only** in the particular context. There will however be **only one answer which matches the question in every single aspect**. If you are not wholly satisfied that your chosen alternative meets this criterion, then it will not be the right one.

Aural exercises

The kind of exam test where comprehension depends on the spoken word may involve one of three written types of response:

multiple choice selection, full answers (in French or English) or reproduction (in French) of a story read aloud.

Whatever is the type which you must face, the over-riding concern must be **absolute concentration** on what is being read. Your reactions have to be virtually instantaneous, as you will only have two (or at most three) opportunities to assimilate the information. The passage will be read as a whole and then broken down into shorter sections on a second reading to enable you to write the answers relating to that section, or read a second time after a short interval during which time you are allowed to make notes. You will need to exercise the same skills as in written comprehension, along with the additional art of keeping a sharp ear open. If you are not familiar with spoken French then you do have a problem, but hopefully this situation is not too widespread these days. There is also some correlation between the attitude required of you in this test and that required for the dictation. You must concentrate hard on what is being said, while at the same time trying to relate each small section to the larger context of the whole passage. In other words, focus on detail but consider this within the total perspective. You are allowed to see the questions (or outline situation to be reproduced) as the reading is proceeding, so you should obviously bear this in mind, keeping on the alert for relevant information and key words and phrases. Finally, just as for a dictation, never bog yourself down with difficulties; leave them temporarily unsolved (you can mull over them later), and keep listening for what is still to come.

The type of exercise where you are required to reproduce the story in your own words will be referred to again later in the essay chapter which follows.

Student answer

Read carefully the following passage. Then without translating it, answer in French the questions following it. (The past historic tense, e.g. je parlai, should not be used in your answers.)

The German police search a flat

Après le départ du chef de la Résistance, je restai seule dans l'appartement. Je rentrai dans le salon.
— Le chef aura peut-être laissé quelques signes de sa visite, me dis-je; des bouts de cigarettes, le télégramme qu'il m'a apporté. Il faut les cacher.
A ce moment-là, justement, un bruit infernal se fit entendre dans

le vestibule. Je me précipitai pour fermer la porte. Trop tard. La
porte s'ouvrait déjà. De toutes mes forces je la poussai, espérant
ainsi gagner les secondes nécessaires pour mettre de l'ordre dans
l'appartement. Inutile. Au moment où j'allais abandonner la lutte
inégale, une voix cria:
– Madame Dupont! Ouvrez: Police allemande!
Je sautai en arrière, et toute une foule d'hommes en uniforme
vert-de-gris entrèrent.
– Où est l'homme? Où est-il? me crièrent-ils.
– Quel homme? dis-je. Je suis une femme seule. Il y a d'autres
appartements dans cette maison. Si vous cherchez quelqu'un,
essayez les autres appartements!
– C'est vrai, dit un officier. Nous perdons du temps. Montons voir.
Gardez-la, dit-il à un petit soldat.
Les soldats sortirent. Le télégramme était au beau milieu de la
table. Il y avait un paquet aussi de mouchoirs en papier. Suivie des
yeux du petit soldat, j'allai vers la table, pris un mouchoir et le
laissai tomber sur le télégramme. Puis je ramassai le tout et
m'essuyai le nez.
– Que puis-je faire de ce télégramme enveloppé dans un mouchoir?
me demandai-je. Le mettre dans mon sac à main? Non, on pourrait
examiner le sac. Dans la corbeille à papier? Non; quand les soldats
reviendront sans avoir trouvé l'homme, ils vont chercher partout . . .
C'est à ce moment-là que le petit soldat vit mon hésitation.
– Jetez-le par la fenêtre, dit-il en riant. Les rues françaises sont si
sales qu'un mouchoir de plus . . .
Et sur la commande d'un soldat allemand je jetai par la fenêtre le
télégramme qui portait la date et le lieu de la grande réunion des
chefs de la Résistance.
Bientôt tous les autres revinrent.
– Il n'est pas là, dit l'officier. Il s'est sauvé. Pourquoi avez-vous
repoussé la porte quand nous avons voulu entrer?
– Mettez-vous à ma place, répondis-je. Vous m'avez fait peur.
D'ailleurs, j'ai ouvert en entendant les mots 'police allemande'.
– Oui, c'est exact. Vous fumez?
Je croyais d'abord qu'il allait m'offrir une cigarette, et j'allais
refuser, mais je me rappelai à temps le paquet de cigarettes dans le
cendrier. L'officier l'avait vu, sans doute.
– Oui, j'adore fumer!
Et je pris une cigarette, l'allumai, et fumai pour la première fois de
ma vie.

1. *Qui avait fait visite à Madame Dupont ce jour-là, et pourquoi?*
2. *Pourquoi Madame Dupont voulait-elle mettre de l'ordre dans*

l'appartement ?

3. *Pourquoi est-ce que les soldats ont quitté l'appartement presque immédiatement ?*
4. *Est-ce qu'ils sont tous partis ?*
5. *Comment Madame Dupont a-t-elle pu ramasser le télégramme sans attirer l'attention du soldat ?*
6. *Pourquoi a-t-elle hésité, le mouchoir à la main ?*
7. *Qu'est-ce qu'elle a fait enfin du mouchoir, et pourquoi ?*
8. *Qu'est-ce que l'officier allemand a voulu savoir quand il est rentré chez Madame Dupont ?*
9. *Pourquoi l'officier allemand a-t-il demandé à Madame Dupont si elle fumait ?*
10. *Adorait-elle vraiment fumer ? Comment le savez-vous ?*

(The Associated Examining Board)

Student answer

1. Le chef de la Résistance avait fait visite à Madame Dupont pour lui donner un télégramme.
2. Madame Dupont voulait mettre de l'ordre dans l'appartement *cacher* les signes de la visite du chef de la Résistance.
3. Les soldats ont quitté l'appartement presque immédiatement pour *chercher* les autres appartements.
4. Non, ils ne sont pas tous partis, un petit soldat *s'est* resté dans *le* appartement.
5. Elle *l'a pu* ramasser en laissant tomber un mouchoir en papier sur le télégramme.
6. Elle a hésité parce qu'elle ne *sait* pas que faire *avec le* télégramme qui était dans le mouchoir.
7. Enfin elle a jeté le mouchoir par *le* fenêtre parce que le petit soldat lui avait *dit le* faire.
8. L'officier allemand a voulu savoir pourquoi elle avait repoussé la porte quand ils ont voulu entrer.
9. Il a demandé à Madame Dupont si elle fumait parce qu'il *a* vu *les* paquet de cigarettes sur la cheminée et les bouts de cigarettes dans le cendrier.
10. Non, elle n'adorait pas fumer parce *qu'il était* la première *fois qu'elle avait fumé dans sa vie.*

1. This is an accurate answer which demonstrates, in addition, correct usage of a concise verbal phrase 'pour+infinitive'.
2. Strange to say, here the candidate has employed a similar

idea, but has omitted the preposition 'pour' to indicate 'in order to'. Although unadventurous in his answer, he has made good use of the original on the whole.

3. 'Chercher' will not suffice to indicate 'to search'. To have used it with a noun+'dans les autres appartements' would have been acceptable, if the verb 'fouiller' were not known. Two improvements to the answer would have been the simple substitution of a direct object pronoun for 'l'appartement'and the addition of an adverbial phrase to indicate the location of the other flats (e.g. '. . . d'en haut' or 'à l'étage supérieur').

4. The two very silly errors in this answer only serve to re-emphasise the need for thorough checking of work – it is so pointless to lose marks in this way. It could also be expected, I think, that the candidate should explain why the soldier stayed behind ('. . . pour garder Madame Dupont').

5. The error made here over the position of object pronouns with an infinitive is a common one. Invariably the pronoun is placed before the verb it logically completes, and invariably this is the infinitive. It is unfortunate that the candidate has made this error, while trying to improve the quality of his answer – this again underlines the point that you must be *sure* of any refinements you add to a basic answer. Full marks however for the use of the present participle here.

6. The use of the idiom 'ne savoir que faire' is neat, but is spoiled by the bad sequence of tense. 'Savait' is the correct tense; it is a pity that the candidate, having selected the idiom, should have failed to apply that slight additional thought process which would have turned the phrase into a real bonus. Incidentally the correct idiom for 'to do (something) with . . .' is 'faire . . . de', not 'avec'. It *is* there in the text.
The end of the answer given here is a good illustration of how a candidate can, quite simply, turn an original phrase into something bearing a more personal stamp ('qui était . . . instead of 'enveloppé dans . . .').

7. Good and bad – the old 'curate's egg'. Good points are the slick and natural-sounding use of pronouns, together with correct transposition of tense to the pluperfect; the omission of 'de' following the 'dire' construction is bad.

8. A good answer; the candidate has fallen into neither of the two areas of possible major error, which are failure to transpose the tense or person of the verbs correctly.

9. Strictly speaking the pluperfect is required again here ('il avait vu . . .') and the remaining error is sheer carelessness.

10. Confusion between the use of 'c'est' and 'il est' is often

found, even at higher exam levels. There are a few 'grey' areas but in the vast majority of cases the situation is clear-cut and all candidates should make a point of learning the distinctions thoroughly. Here is an example of a clear-cut case; a sense of definition is involved, thus 'c'est . . . que . . .'. Correct French usage would have been to finish the phrase in this way, '. . . la première fois de sa vie qu'elle fumait'.

In total this is a very respectable answer. You can see for yourself that, generally speaking, the candidate has not been too ambitious as concerns the personal expression of the information contained in the text. There is evidence to suggest that the candidate can handle pronouns and tenses quite well and can manipulate the language reasonably effectively, within the framework of well tried structures. Such qualities are admirable; a cautious approach is infinitely preferable to the wildly individual (and wildly inaccurate) line of action. You must **never sacrifice accuracy to eccentricity**, and should stick to the maxim 'If you don't know how to say it, don't!'

Common errors

The errors which spring from rushing to put pen to paper have already been mentioned (**repeating information, giving unnecessary details**). You should have enough time, so make use of it. Careful reading always repays the time taken.

Copying large sections of the text wholesale impresses nobody, and will do nothing for you. Most often, in any case, this will be disastrous from a grammatical point of view, since the examination questions are purposely contrived so as to force you to manipulate tenses, persons, pronouns, etc., to produce a correct answer.

Two types of question lead the 'too trusting' candidate (or maybe the thoughtless one!) into error almost more often than any others. These are the ones beginning 'Qui . . .?' and 'Combien de . . .?' 'Qui' as subject is necessarily followed by a singular verb form, but the answer may very well involve more than one person. 'Combien de . . .', on the other hand, is necessarily followed by a plural verb form, but of course the answer here may well involve a singular response. Thinking before you write should prevent you making these errors. You should not allow the fact that you are very likely to be using the same verb as in the question to lure you into thinking the ending on that verb will necessarily also be the same.

Many candidates are caught out in the situation where a **noun idea needs to be turned into a verb**, or a **preposition into a conjunction**, or the other way round. 'Ringing at doorbells', 'knocking on doors', 'telephoning', are classic examples, as are 'because' *v.* 'because *of*', 'since', and other troublesome little words. You really have to realise, and the quicker the better, that there is no noun that can be made from 'sonner' to mean a 'ring at the door', nor from 'frapper' to mean 'a knock at the door'. The use of 'un coup' (de sonnette, à la porte) is after all by no means uncommon, nor are the very many other expressions ('un coup de pied, de tête, de poing', etc.) which employ this basic noun. All of these are favourite targets of examiners: make sure you can handle them with confidence.

Changes from direct to indirect speech give rise to many errors of tense and we have seen examples in this very chapter. Really the situation is precisely as in English; both tenses and persons of the verb are going to be affected by this change. Unfortunately it seems necessary to point out in addition that the basic requirement for **each clause** is a **finite verb** (i.e. *not* an infinitive form). Such a mistake as 'il manger' is appalling. As in other chapters it is appropriate to repeat that any and **every form of grammatical aberration** is found in comprehension exercises of the kind we have discussed here. Literally everything from adjective agreements to compound tenses seems to attract the careless candidate. We have also seen from our student answer that pronouns really are a vulnerable area, but authentic language cannot be created without recourse to them.

Where answers are required in English candidates fail, alas, by their **inability to express themselves in clear and correct English**, by their poor or sloppy style of writing, and by their spelling mistakes. To squander marks by falling down on standards of presentation and the grammar of one's native tongue is unbelievably stupid.

As for aurally conducted tests, candidates sometimes fail to appreciate the **time/opportunity factor** which is obviously limited to a considerable degree. The key to success is concentration on the relevant section at the relevant time. There is normally ample time allowed for the average candidate, so don't panic!

Essay

It is, perhaps, unfortunate that the terms 'essay' or 'composition' seem to suggest grandiose achievement, since that is the opposite of what is required in an O-level French examination. The purpose of this exercise is to test the candidate's ability to express himself accurately in written form on an everyday topic. Increasingly these days the context is limited both in length and scope, in an attempt to eliminate some of the worst horrors of non-French drivel produced by the majority of candidates if given greater freedom. Therefore, although a very small percentage of candidates will find the new essay formats restricting, their structured framework is certainly in the interests of the majority.

There are several possible types of essay, and each has to be accomplished in 100–150 words, depending on individual examining Boards. There is a tendency towards two contrasting exercises; you may be required to write on the basis of two of the following stimulus patterns:
(a) story outline or set situation;
(b) picture series;
(c) continuation of a story (possibly encountered as a translation passage or aural exercise), *OR* reproduction of a story read aloud;
(d) letter (formal or informal);
(e) account of a simple adventure or incident (possibly to be expressed as a dialogue).

Model answers

Write approximately 150 words in French, telling the story suggested by the series of pictures opposite.
(*This story idea might also have been expressed as a suggested outline, as follows:*
Une jeune fille gagne le Gros Lot – elle part en vacances – elle passe des vacances merveilleuses – elle rencontre un jeune homme riche – au retour en France elle achète encore un billet de loterie.)

Model answer (A)
Unforgettable holidays
Maryvonne ne pouvait en croire ses yeux : elle venait de gagner le Gros Lot à la Loterie Nationale. Tout de suite elle est allée à

72

l'agence de voyage où elle a choisi des vacances à Madagascar. La veille du départ elle a fait tous ses préparatifs. A Madagascar il faisait un temps superbe. Après s'être installée dans une belle chambre qui donnait sur la mer, elle a couru à la plage. Bientôt un beau jeune homme lui a parlé et – quelle chance! – il l'a invitée ce soir-là à une surprise-partie à bord son yacht. Là elle a dansé et bu du champagne toute la soirée.

Hélas – trop vite les vacances étaient finies. Désolée, Maryvonne a dû retourner en France. En arrivant à l'aéroport, elle a remarqué un kiosque où elle a dépensé ses derniers francs pour . . . un billet de la Loterie Nationale. (*148 words*)

Imagine that you are Henri and write in French, in about 100 words, an answer to this letter:

Lyon, le 12 décembre

Mon cher Henri,

Je suis vraiment content d'apprendre que tu pourras venir passer la fête de Noël chez nous. Veux-tu m'écrire aussitôt que possible, s'il te plaît, pour me dire si ta sœur t'accompagnera. Je voudrais savoir aussi le jour de ton arrivée; il faudra que Catherine fasse ses achats bien à l'avance. Si tu me dis par quel train tu arriveras, j'irai te prendre à la gare.

En attendant le plaisir de te lire,

Ton ami,
Michel
(The Associated Examining Board)

Paris, le 15 décembre

Model answer (B)

Mon cher Michel,

Merci beaucoup de ta lettre. Voilà les renseignements que tu m'as demandés. Malheureusement Suzanne ne pourra pas m'accompagner chez toi; elle va passer quinze jours à faire du ski. (L'année dernière elle s'est beaucoup amusée mais il n'a pas neigé du tout!)

Je compte arriver chez toi le soir du mercredi vingt-trois; si je prenais le train de cinq heures et demie, je devrais être à Lyon vers neuf heures. Tu es gentil de venir me chercher à la gare – ma valise sera lourde de cadeaux!

Amicalement,
Henri (*101 words*)

A friend with whom you have lost touch calls on you unexpectedly, after seeing a photograph of you in a newspaper. Imagine your conversation; how the friend came to be in the district, what you both have done since you last met and what your future plans are. Write your dialogue in about 150 words.

Model answer (C)

Mireille: Tiens! Jeannine! – quelle surprise!

Jeannine: Bonjour Mireille. Quel plaisir de te revoir!

Mireille: Mais que fais-tu ici? Je te croyais en Allemagne. Cela fait deux ans que nous ne nous sommes pas vues, non?

Jeannine: En effet je suis à Hambourg depuis deux ans, mais je suis revenue pour le mariage de mon frère dimanche prochain. Hier en lisant le journal j'ai remarqué ta photo – avec la Coupe de tennis! Bravo!

Mireille: Malgré mon travail je fais toujours beaucoup de sport. A propos, savais-tu que je suis infirmière? Autrefois je voulais devenir hôtesse de l'air, mais j'ai changé d'avis – on m'a dit comme c'était fatigant.

Jeannine: Avant d'aller à Hambourg j'ai passé six mois en voyage. Je resterai encore un an là-bas, puis je serai contente d'être professeur – peut-être!

Mireille: Tu pourras passer toute la soirée avec nous, j'espère?

Jeannine: Avec plaisir. (149 *words*)

Answer plan

Write approximately 150 words in French, telling the story depicted in the series of pictures over the page.

If you have chosen this alternative, then one must assume that you are quite able to deal with the likely vocabulary items. The picture outline contains all the basic information for your account – you need not, however, gnash your teeth in angry frustration at restriction of your creative talent: you are not, after all, out to make the best-seller list. This apparent strait-jacket will enable you to concentrate on writing accurate French and will stop you indulging in flights of imagination which you could not possibly render in a foreign language.

Planning is essential: you must cover all the points mentioned within a given word limit – the excess will not be marked, and the more you write, the more mistakes you are likely to make. Whichever essay format you are following (picture, outline, dialogue, etc.), there will be a number of points to be made.

76

For this reason it is a good idea to **plan your work in paragraphs** corresponding to these points (or to the pictures, if this is the case). For each paragraph you should note down **key words or phrases** which you will want to bring in. It has already been stressed that accuracy must be the first consideration. Candidates should also remember, however, that, while this quality on its own will be enough to gain good marks, it will need to be supplemented by some further elaboration to earn first-class credit. This need mean nothing daunting – judicious use of pronouns, a good range of tenses, introduction of verb constructions such as 'demander à quelqu'un de faire quelque chose', and so on; in other words evidence that the candidate can express himself in normal, natural French. In everyday language you come across sentences of varying lengths, and not just the simple subject+verb+object pattern seen all too frequently in examination scripts. Subordinate clauses are not difficult but demonstrate the variety which helps to gain a candidate marks.

Let us apply this planning procedure to the composition here, noting down the essential vocabulary points:

Picture 1: faire de l'auto-stop – au bord de la route – (Nice) à 250 kilomètres – faire du soleil.

Picture 2: une voiture – un paysage de montagne – parler avec le conducteur.

Picture 3: prendre un verre – la terrasse d'un café.

Picture 4: tomber en panne – loin de— – regarder le moteur – commencer à pleuvoir.

Picture 5: pousser la voiture – difficile – pleuvoir beaucoup.

Picture 6: une station-service – une affiche – recommander un voyage en train – plus rapide.

The suggestions here are elementary and provided there were no gross errors, it should prove possible for any candidate who is considered O-level material to produce, even from this bony skeleton, an acceptable though uninspiring composition. Just such a version might be the following:

Un jour deux jeunes gens faisaient de l'auto-stop au bord de la route. Ils voulaient aller à Nice, à deux cents cinquante kilomètres. Il faisait du soleil.
Une voiture s'est arrêtée, et bientôt ils étaient dans un paysage de montagnes. Ils ont parlé avec le conducteur. A onze heures ils ont pris un verre à la terrasse d'un café; ils ont commandé de l'eau minérale.
Après quelque temps sur la route la voiture est tombée en panne,

loin d'une ville. Le conducteur a regardé le moteur, les jeunes
ont regardé le conducteur ; il a commencé à pleuvoir.
Les trois personnes ont poussé la voiture. C'était difficile et
maintenant il pleuvait beaucoup.
Heureusement ils ont vu une station-service. Sur la route aussi
il y avait une affiche qui recommandait les voyages en train.
'Oui,' pensaient les jeunes gens, 'c'est plus rapide'. (149 *words*)

You could plan to do much better than this by a variety of fairly
simple expedients. You could be much less rigid with your sentence structure; you could add an adjective or adverb, or verb
construction; you could link clauses, and so on. Here are some
suggestions for one way in which it could be achieved.

Picture 1: Vocabulary: – par un beau matin d'été – un auto-
stoppeur – attendre au bord de la route. You could reduce the
paragraph to a single sentence, by introducing a participle
phrase to express the young people's intention (=voulant aller
. . .).

Picture 2: Vocabulary: – être là depuis+time – bavarder – un
paysage montagneux. You could add a suitable adjective to
describe the driver (=aimable) and you could again combine two
ideas by using a present participle construction (=en traversant
un paysage . . .).

Picture 3: Vocabulary; – vers 11 heures – décidé de (prendre un
verre). You could add a short phrase to describe the location of
the café (=dans un village pittoresque).

Picture 4: Vocabulary: – repartir – un endroit isolé. You could
supply an adjective (=joyeux) to describe their mood as they set
off again, and in the obvious places you could insert 'soudain',
'en vain', 'malheureusement' or 'hélas'.

Picture 5: Vocabulary: – que faire? – en haut de la colline –
pleuvoir à verse. You could turn the idea of it being a hard task
into an adverbial phrase (=avec difficulté), and perhaps use the
simple phrase 'tous les trois' to add variety.

Picture 6: Vocabulary: – trempé jusqu'aux os – une affiche
publicitaire – en effet. A neat way to combine the ideas contained
in the original first two sentences of the last paragraph at the top
of this page would be to use the past participle phrase (=arrivés
dans une station-service). There is also a good opportunity to
express the idea 'we should have . . .' (=nous aurions dû+
infinitive).

It undoubtedly requires considerable ingenuity and thought to
make good use of 100–150 words, but that is exactly the point!

You can see from the 'plain' version given on the previous pages that in fact there are quite a number of phrases used which waste words and the simple repetitive sentence formulae do not help at all with the question of getting your money's worth. The well structured sentence is invariably the more concise and thus provides a little extra space for the insertion of the additional adjective or descriptive phrase which will earn you marks. Just one word of warning – candidates who produce a string of idioms which have no relevance to the composition in question must expect to be penalised for this. Write on what is there but *never* on what is not!

Finally in this section, a few hints on the particular requirements of a composition in dialogue or letter form, or one reproducing a story read aloud.

(a) **Dialogue:** you should plan the points to be made in the same way as for a narrative story (see Model Answer C), noting relevant key phrases before you begin to write. Above all you must avoid the senseless padding that often produces the worst examples of scripts. By this I mean the following:

A: Bonjour, B, comment allez-vous?
B: Très bien, merci, et vous?
A: Très bien merci. Il fait beau aujourd'hui, n'est-ce pas?
B: Oui, il fait beau . . . etc., etc.

This represents 24 wasted words and is by no means as bad as it might be – at least here the French is accurate. You simply have no time or space to waste on twaddle – you are asked to make a number of specific points and must get on with them.

With both the dialogue and the letter it is, of course, essential that the **main past tense is the perfect**; with both, also, the question of **tu/vous forms** (with their associated adjectives and pronouns) takes on special importance. It will be inevitable that these forms are involved but the elementary decision as to whether 'tu' or 'vous' is appropriate for the tone and type of dialogue or letter seems, alas, to be ignored disturbingly often. Contrary to popular belief, these essay forms are by no means easy options and if you do not discipline yourself to put all the above points into practice, you will undoubtedly produce a poor answer.

(b) **Letter:** an important supplementary point to the ones just outlined concerns the formulae for beginning and ending letters. You are not expected to be familiar with a vast range of the almost endless possibilities of etiquette respected by the French in the matter of letter writing. You must know, of course, how to distinguish between informal and formal terminology and how to reply accordingly. For example, you do *not* address a hotel manager as 'tu', nor do you send him 'love and kisses' (=grosses bises) at the end of your letter! It has been done – very often, and very recently . . . .

(c) **Reproduction of a story read aloud:** the main facility you will require in this exercise is speedy reactions. By the nature of the exercise it does not bear the same onus of planning as the other composition types. You must, therefore, concentrate on the key words or phrases you *hear*, and as soon as writing is permitted, write these down, including (if there is one) the final punch line. In theory this exercise cuts out many of the areas for potential error since you are working from a perfect model answer. You will, in fact, succeed in doing this in practice if you are well enough prepared for what is coming along. **Listen to the tense of the verbs used** as these will need to be imitated in your version. You are *not* required to be inventive, and although your account will doubtlesss be simpler, the more aware you are of exactly what has been read to you, the closer you are likely to come to a correct rendering of the original. This is not simply a case of 'being able to do it or not' – most candidates are not specially gifted, and the ones who succeed are simply the ones who make the effort and concentrate. Of course, general ability will sort out good and bad candidates but there again it is more likely to be the degree of effort they manifest which largely accounts for the success of the better candidates.

Student answer

Do not write out the following paragraph but, starting from the point reached at its end, continue the story in French, using about 150 words. State at the end the number of words you have used.

Un jour faisiez une promenade à la campagne lorsque vous avez remarqué quelque chose par terre qui brillait. Vous vous êtes baissé(e) pour mieux voir . . .

Student answer

(1) *Il y avait* sept pièces de monnaie, trois en argent et quatre en or. Je les ai *ramassé* et je les ai *frotté* avec les

mains. Elles étaient couvertes de *sol*. J'ai cru qu'elles étaient très anciennes et je suis allée chez moi, *pour* les *monter* à ma mère *et mon père*. *Ils étaient très intéressés*.

(2) Ma mère *a apporté une toile* et j'ai essayé *à* enlever *le sol*. Bientot *j'ai pu* voir la date *des monnaie*. C'était dix-huit *cents* vingt-cinq. J'ai mis la monnaie dans une petite boîte et mon *pére m'a* conduit au musée.

(3) J'ai dit *le portier* que j'avais trouvé sept pièces de monnaie et *il m'a pris* au professeur. Le professeur a nettoyé la monnaie puis il a regardé *dans* un microscope. Il était très stupéfié parce qu'il avait *découvri* que la monnaie *étaient* très précieux.

(4) Il m'a demandé s'il *garderais* la monnaie. Maintenant la monnaie est dans le musée avec mon nom à côté.

(173 *words*)

Comments This is a fairly carefully written composition, but it also contains some typical errors. In general terms it lacks that structural polish mentioned earlier in the chapter which would have turned it into a first-class answer, even supposing the grammatical faults were eliminated. It is also too long, unnecessarily so, by the way, as we shall see later on. **An excess of up to ten words** is tolerable, but where there are twenty or more, as here, they will be ignored, which is unfortunate if they contain an idea which rounds off the story.

(1) The composition starts rather abruptly and the over-used phrase 'il y avait' certainly gives it no great panache. 'Se trouver' is almost always more acceptable, and of course there are several other good alternatives, depending on the context.

je les ai ramassé: the candidate has forgotten the preceding direct object agreement both here and with the subsequent verb. This sentence could also have been improved stylistically by using the 'après avoir . . .' construction for the first part and thus, incidentally, economising on one word, 'et'.

sol: the word 'la terre' should have been used, 'le sol' conveying more the idea of 'ground' than of 'earth'.

In the following sentence, a little extra polish could easily have been added by substituting the phrase 'Je les croyais très anciennes' or 'Elles devaient être très anciennes'.

pour: this is unnecessary following the verb 'aller' which suggests 'go and do . . .' This sentence is completed by two very typical errors:

(a) confusion between the verbs 'monter' and 'montrer'; (b) omission of the preposition 'à' before 'mon père' (and in any case why not 'à mes parents'?) All of the corrections from this section have the merit of conciseness into the bargain.

Ils . . . intéressés: This sentence is a total disaster, and it is not worth dwelling on its individual component errors. The phrase 'to be interested in' is very much standard O-level fare, and is almost bound to figure in the oral exam at least; candidates therefore *must* know how to express the idea in French, 'S'intéresser à . . .' is the basic formula, together with the other idiom 'prendre beaucoup d'intérêt à . . .', which would have well suited this situation. (It would be wise to revise thoroughly the use of object pronouns in connection with verbs such as these which include a preposition.)

(2) *a apporté une toile*: 'aller chercher' would have been much more appropriate a verb here, since 'apporter' suggests 'to bring from another location' – much too purposeful.

une toile: it would be unlikely! Used with the indefinite article it rather implies 'an oil painting' or 'a canvas'. The idea is obviously simply 'a cloth', but 'la toile' used in this sense refers principally to a type of material (=linen cloth). What is needed is 'un chiffon'.

essayé à: wrong preposition. It is vital to have these well learnt so that use becomes instinctive.

The candidate has used the verb 'pouvoir' quite logically in connection with the idea 'can see'. It is, however, worth pointing out that it is not necessary to use 'pouvoir' in this connection (nor with the idea 'can hear'). 'Je voyais' or 'j'entendais' both adequately convey the idea.

des monnaie: 'des pièces de monnaie' is correct. The noun 'la monnaie' about which there is endless confusion, notably with 'l'argent', is a collective noun (=change, or currency).

dix-huit cents: no candidate should lose marks on inaccuracies of numbers, dates, times, but alas! many always do so each year. Look up the rules for agreement of 'cent', 'mille', 'demi', etc., if you do not see the error here.

The last sentence of this section is grammatically accurate but reading it one has the feeling it is not a very satisfactory one. The candidate could probably have produced something much more pleasing which would have been less dependent on the reader's deducing an intermediary step between the two halves of the sentence. A possible alternative could be: 'Ayant mis les pièces de monnaie dans une petite boîte, j'ai persuadé mon père de me conduire au musée.'

(3) – *dire le portier*: 'dire *à*+object'. It can only be re-emphasised how important and fundamental to good language usage are constructions using this pattern. ('Le concierge' would have been a more appropriate choice of noun in any case here.) By this time the constant repetition of 'sept pièces de monnaie' is becoming decidedly monotonous, and suggests their rightful place might possibly be in a children's fairy story! A much neater variant here would be 'ce que j'avais trouvé'.

il m'a pris: 'prendre' is another oft mis-used word. It is *not* used to indicate 'to take someone along somewhere' – this is the verb 'emmener'. The idea associated with 'prendre' is always one of physical contact (picking something up, taking someone by the arm, in one's arms, etc. – i.e. touching the object or beneficiary!). We also know from a previous agreement ('je suis allée chez moi') that the candidate is female, and so the examiner would, of course, insist again on the preceding direct object agreement being indicated on the end of the past participle (=emmenée). This may sound tough luck on the poor girl, since the problem would not have arisen with a boy candidate, but if you indicate something about yourself in your work, then you have to remain consistent.

Le professeur . . . un microscope: again not a 'bad' sentence, ('dans un microscope' should be rendered 'au microscope', but that is not terribly serious). But it is a boring sentence – one might say it is 'baby French'! Why repeat 'le professeur' when 'celui-ci' would be so much better? Why stick to the trusty old formula of two clauses joined by 'et'? We have already seen examples of how this linguistic rut can be avoided.

The same criticism applies also to the following sentence. It does not require genius to alter this to advantage. To begin the sentence with the adjective 'Stupéfié . . .' is a great improvement, and I would hardly think the adverb 'très' is useful here in any case. It would also be better to work along the lines 'il m'a appris que . . .' (=he informed me that . . .), rather than to choose the verb 'découvrir' – past participle 'décou*vert*'! The professor has not discovered anything in the true meaning of the word.

que la monnaie étaient précieux: feminine noun+plural verb +masculine adjective agreement! Oh dear! Something obviously has to alter radically!

(4) *s'il garderais*: the mistake in verb ending is a bad one, but the

83

mistake in tense can expect a more sympathetic response. 'S'il pouvait garder' is correct; the imperfect must in any case replace the conditional, since 'si=if' can never be followed by future or conditional tenses.

The final phrase could, I feel, have been rather more striking with very little additional effort ('au musée' is much more idiomatic than 'dans le musée', by the way). The use of a relative clause, for instance, to avoid repeating the noun 'la monnaie' would be one idea. One possibility for a simple conclusion which would nevertheless offer slightly more punch might be '. . . qui est maintenant au musée. Allez la voir – et vous verrez mon nom à côté'.

Final comments, therefore, are that this is a 'safe' composition and one must conclude that the candidate had no aspirations to a first-class answer. That is, of course, a perfectly legitimate ambition and it cannot be pointed out too strongly that examiners would be all too delighted if the majority of candidates worked in accordance with such an aim, and produced safe, accurate accounts. But I think this candidate's general standard seems to suggest she did not maximise her potential. On the credit side, the handling of tenses is above average (apart from one or two catastrophes). Therefore it could reasonably be assumed that this area did not present her with great problems. Yet we see very little evidence of anything other than the perfect tense – the candidate should have been more ingenious in showing off a few other tenses. The examiner cannot, after all, award marks for what he suspects the candidate *might* know. What you write is what he will mark, so you really have to work at producing a script which does justice to your ability and knowledge. In this exercise perhaps more than in any of the others (except the oral exam), it is very much up to you to find ways of **showing off what you know**. If, of course, you don't know much, then – fair enough – keep it simple and correct, and keep the examiner guessing about the real extent of your knowledge!

Comment has already been passed on the excessively simple sentence structure, which is not going to bring the candidate any credit. The same lack of imagination can also be criticised in another area, namely that of vocabulary. This is to be seen, despite the one or two slightly less common words ('frotter', 'stupéfié'), in the general lack of adjectives, adverbs and conjunctions. There are very few, and again one suspects this is not because none are known, but merely because the candidate has not thought hard enough about how they might be introduced. In general terms the vocabulary is both repetitive and unexciting. Whereas it should go without saying that trying to say what you do not know how to express is sheer lunacy – do *not* forget that it really annoys an examiner dreadfully to be faced with made-up nonsense – it is in your best interests to manipulate as cleverly as you can what you *do* know. That must be the principal reservation about this candidate – one has the impression that here she has not produced an answer which reflects adequately her probable level of understanding and general potential.

Common errors

All reports from the examining Boards comment on the **length** of candidates' essays. There simply is **no point at all in exceeding the stated limit.** This is repeating what has already been said in this chapter, but the criticism is an annual one, and therefore does need to be stressed. If part of your essay is not going to be marked (which is the usual practice for dealing with over-long offerings), the section which *is* marked is unlikely to be complete, or to have covered all the points asked for. It is probable, too, that you have been longwinded in what you have written for it to have needed three hundred words (or more), while other candidates have managed to express themselves succinctly in the prescribed 150. So you are penalising yourself doubly; now add to that a third penalty – lack of accuracy. The more you scribble away feverishly, the less attentive you will be to the quality and accuracy of what you are writing. **Don't do it!** Examiners also comment each year on **irrelevance** – candidates who are guilty of this are either the hopelessly inadequate who pad out their account with nonsense (and who are thus insulting the examiner's intelligence – not a recommended course of action!); or those who think themselves frightfully clever and introduce a phrase-book collection of **idioms** which have **nothing at all to do with the subject matter** of the composition. Such a candidate would doubtless sit preening his feathers after penning the following: 'Après s'être saoulé comme un Polonais la veille au soir, Jean, au bout de son rouleau, n'était pas dans son assiette, et ne voulait rien faire que la grasse matinée . . ., etc. Idioms and neat turns of phrase are splendid *provided* they fit the context. It is simply no good learning idioms which you are determined to bring in at all costs. If it were a game of 'Consequences' the situation could be quite hilarious, but it is not! The question of irrelevance suggests a lack of self-discipline and this can reveal itself in a further common fault – **failure to make some of the points requested** in the instructions, or (in the case of a picture series) not commenting on what is there. It is no use bursting to express your own individuality if it does not take account of the instructions you are working to.

It is fatal to think in English and translate. Your thoughts expressed in your own language are bound to be more sophisticated than your French and you will only heap a store of disasters upon yourself if you follow this line. At O-level the examiner is not primarily interested in your literary talent – he is interested in the way in which you can organise the fruits of five years' study into concise, accurate statements relating to a given theme. So accept as a golden rule that you **contain your composition within the limits of your linguistic experience.**

Concerning the precise details of grammatical inaccuracies, once again the field is boundless. The main areas which have been examined in previous chapters are the chief culprits here too, (tense errors, verbal atrocities, pronouns, agreements, etc.). The only difference in this exercise is that all are likely to be worse! The candidate is dividing his attention between what he wants to say and the constraints of a foreign language, and time after time, he will bend what in his heart of hearts he knows to be correct in order to accommodate a particular idea he simply must express – very often something which is intended to be a pun. It rarely works. It is therefore of the utmost importance that the candidate makes a real attempt to counter this danger, by **checking** most particularly **all he writes**, using the checking system given on pages 50–1. The moral, therefore, of this tale is: if it fails to meet the needs of the check list, or if you actually know what you want to put down is wrong – do not succumb to temptation!

The Examination Paper

In this final section of the book the aim is to reproduce as closely as possible an example of a full examination paper, as attempted by one candidate. This will preclude both the oral and dictation tests, and also the listening comprehension exercises, partly on the grounds of limited available space and partly on the grounds of feasibility. A scripted version of a fifteen-minute oral exam is obviously unrealistic, as is a listening comprehension test, and the dictation contains nothing which is open to interpretation or improvement. It is nevertheless assumed that all three exercises form part of the exam and that the weighting for the different exercises is as follows:

Paper I:	Dictation	15 marks =	$7\frac{1}{2}\%$
Paper II:	1. Translation into English	40 marks =	$\left.\rule{0pt}{2.5ex}\right\}30\%$
	2. Listening comprehension	20 marks =	
Paper III:	1. Written comprehension	40 marks =	$\left.\rule{0pt}{2.5ex}\right\}37\frac{1}{2}\%$
	2. Essay	35 marks =	
Paper IV:	Oral	50 marks =	25%
		TOTAL =	100%

This selection of exercises is intended to be representative of present examination trends, rather than of the style of one particular Board. Since the section for translation into French is becoming a less favoured exercise, it has been omitted.

Paper II: Section 1

Translate into English

*C'était l'heure maintenant où le collège se vidait pour trois mois.
Les enfants avaient pris congé de leurs maîtres, les familles avaient
pris congé du Directeur du collège. La foule qui descendait lente-
ment les escaliers allait gagner la cour, la rue, la gare. Un sourd
bruit informait le Père Denis de ce qui se passait. Un grand silence
allait s'étendre bientôt sur tout le collège, un silence qui le remplissait toujours de mélancolie. A ce moment retentit dans le
couloir le son d'une galopade. La porte fut ouverte brusquement et
trois élèves essouflés entrèrent. C'était Poussin, Le Grand et
Martin. Ils s'écrièrent d'une seule voix – On est vite venu vous dire
adieu Père Denis! A l'année prochaine! Bonnes vacances! On vous
aime bien, vous savez, Père Denis! – Cela crié de tout leur coeur, ils
retournèrent en galopant vers les familles.*

*Le Père Denis resta debout, tout seul, pensif, devant sa table. Il en
avait bien vu passer, depuis tant d'années, des élèves. Et toujours
ceux, qui, à l'heure de partir avaient eu pour lui un souvenir, avaient
été les mêmes, les mauvais élèves comme ces trois-là. Le Père
réfléchit pendant quelques instants. Peut-on dire que des enfants
turbulents et moqueurs, parce qu'ils sont vifs et spontanés, sont
mauvais? Mais non. C'est absurde! Le Père sourit, se rassit à la
table et se mit à travailler.*

(Southern Universities Joint Board)

It was now the time when the college emptied for three
months. The children said goodbye to their masters, the
families said goodbye to the College Director. The crowd
which was slowly going down the stairs was going to reach
the yard, the street, the station. A noise informed the
Father Denis about what was passing by. A large silence
was soon going to be heard over all the college, a silence
which always used to fill him with melancholy.

At this moment a galloping noise was heard in the corridor.
The door opened suddenly and three dishevelled pupils
came in. It was Poussin, Le Grand and Martin. They
shouted with a single voice – we have quickly come to say
goodbye Father Denis. To next year. Good holidays to
you! We love you a lot, you know, Father Denis – That
shout came from all their hearts, and they returned at a
gallop towards their families.

The Father Denis remained standing all alone, pensive,

before his table. He had seen some good ones go by out of the pupils, for such a lot of years. And always those who, at the time of leaving had a memory to share with him, were the same, the bad pupils like these three, there. The Father reflected for a few minutes. Can one say that some turbulent and mocking children, because they are alive and spontaneous, are bad? But no! It is absurd. The Father laughed, sat down at the table and began to work.

Paper III : Section 1

Read carefully the following passage. Then, without translating it, answer in French the questions following it. The past historic tense should not be used in your answers.

Helpful Albert

Couché sur son petit lit de camp dans sa cabine, Albert ne pouvait pas dormir.

– C'est la pluie qui bat les murs de la cabine, se dit-il. Si je n'avais pas tellement faim, peut-être que je m'endormirais, malgré le bruit. Soudain, il entendit trois petits coups frappés à la porte. C'était le signal auquel il reconnaissait son nouvel ami Jules.

– Jules, à cette heure-ci? Qu'est-ce qu'il peut bien vouloir? se demanda-t-il. Il se leva et ouvrit la porte. C'était bien Jules, sans chapeau, sans imperméable, et une grande valise à la main.

– Jules! Tu pars? Au milieu de la nuit? Entre donc. Qu'est-ce qu'il y a?

– La police me cherche, répondit Jules. On a trouvé le diamant de Madame Nogent dans ma chambre, et on pense que c'est moi qui l'ai volé. C'est la femme de chambre qui l'a trouvé, et elle a couru appeler la police. Moi, je n'ai pas attendu: j'ai jeté quelques affaires dans la valise, et je suis sorti par la fenêtre.

– Mais pourquoi es-tu venu chez moi? demanda Albert. Tu sais que je ne peux te cacher.

– Non, je vais partir tout de suite. Seulement, je n'ai pas le sou. Prête-moi quelques francs, pour acheter un billet de chemin de fer.

– Comment, tu n'as pas d'argent? s'écria Albert, étonné. Mais tu couches dans le meilleur hôtel, tu connais tous les riches – des gens à qui moi, je n'ose même pas parler.

Jules ne dit rien. Albert, de plus en plus indigné, reprit:

– Aujourd'hui je n'ai pas mangé parce que j'ai acheté un livre qu'il me fallait pour mes études! De l'argent, moi?

– Pauvre gars, dit enfin Jules, je sais que si tu avais deux sous tu me les donnerais. Alors je pars, mais Dieu sait où . . . La gare sera pleine de gendarmes.

– *La voiture de Max est devant la porte, dit Albert. Je vais la . . .*
emprunter, et je te conduirai jusqu'à la prochaine gare. Ils ne
penseront pas à surveiller toutes les gares de la région. A deux
heures du matin, Jules et Albert sortirent à pas furtifs sous la pluie,
montèrent dans la voiture de Max, et partirent sans allumer les phares.
– *Au revoir, Albert, dit Jules en descendant de la voiture. N'attends*
pas. Rentre vite; Max peut s'apercevoir de l'absence de sa voiture.
– *Au revoir Jules, et fais bien attention, n'est-ce pas?*
– *Oh, j'allais oublier, Albert. Tes allumettes; voilà!*
Et Jules jeta une boîte d'allumettes sur la banquette à côté d'Albert,
et puis il disparut dans la nuit.
Albert était à plusieurs kilomètres de là quand il pensa soudain:
– *Mais je n'ai pas donné d'allumettes à Jules! Il arrêta la voiture et*
ouvrit la petite boîte. Il n'y avait pas d'allumettes, mais un gros
diamant brillait dans les rayons de la lune, car il avait cessé de
pleuvoir.

1. *Pourquoi Albert ne pouvait-il pas dormir cette nuit-là?*
2. *Comment savait-il que c'était Jules à la porte?*
3. *Pourquoi Albert s'est-il étonné de l'arrivée de Jules et de son*
   apparence?
4. *Pourquoi est-ce que la police cherchait Jules?*
5. *Qu'est-ce que Jules venait demander, et pourquoi cette demande*
   a-t-elle étonné Albert?
6. *Est-ce qu'Albert avait de l'argent? Comment le savez-vous?*
7. *Pourquoi fallait-il prendre une voiture?*
8. *Qu'est-ce que Jules et Albert ont fait à deux heures du matin?*
9. *Pourquoi est-ce qu'Albert n'a pas attendu le train avec son*
   camarade?
10. *Au retour, pourquoi Albert a-t-il arrêté la voiture?*

(The Associated Examining Board – abbreviated)

1. Parce qu'il pleuvait.
2. Il a entendu trois petits coups frappés à la porte.
3. Parce que Jules était sans chapeau et sans imperméable au milieu de la nuit.
4. Parce que la police a trouvé le diamant de Madame Nogent dans sa chambre.
5. Il venait demander quelques francs. Albert était étonné parce que Jules était riche.
6. Non, il n'en avait pas. Je sais parce que il n'a pas mangé ce jour.
7. Parce qu'ils ne pouvaient pas aller à la gare qui sera

plein de gendarmes.

8. Ils sont sortis à pas furtifs sous la pluie, ils sont montés dans la voiture de Max, et partirent sans allumer les phares.

9. Parce que Max peut s'apercevoir de l'absence de sa voiture.

10. Parce qu'il n'a pas donné des allumetes à Jules.

Section 2: Composition

Write an essay of about 150 words on one of the following subjects. At the end of your essay you should indicate the number of words you have written.

(*a*) *Vous avez travaillé pendant les vacances de Noël dans un grand magasin. Racontez comment cela s'est passé.*

(*b*) *Beginning at the point reached at the end of this paragraph, continue the story:*

Avec un(e) ami(e) vous vous promeniez en ville quand soudain vous avez vu un homme prendre le sac à main à une vieille dame et s'enfuir. 'Au voleur' a-t-elle crié . . .

(*c*) *Ecrivez une conversation qui commence: 'Papa, j'ai quelque chose à te dire.'*

(b) Mon ami et moi avons décidé d'aller au poste de police, pour les dire environ l'homme, mais il courait très vite. Nous avons commencé courir après lui et sur le route j'ai remarqué quatre garçons, qui je connais. Ils sont très forts et tout de suite je les ai demandé de m'aider.

Ils ont dit qu'ils courraient très vite pour l'attraper. Soudain l'homme a tourné et il a vu mes cinq amis et moi. Nous avons continué le chasser. Après quinze minutes il était très fatigué et il s'est arrêté, pour prendre l'air. Un de mes amis, qui est coureur, a continué courir et il a réussi de passer près de lui. L'autres garçons l'ont entourés.Le vouleur n'a pu pas s'évader. Il a tombé le sac sur le trottoir et je suis allé au agent qui dirigeait le traffic. Il a attrapé le voleur et l'a pris au prison.

Enfin j'ai donné sain et sauf le sac à la dame. (*176 words*)

Comments
Translation into English

There are not a tremendous number of really bad errors in this script, but the general tone is rather stilted, with the result that it does not read as natural English throughout. This candidate would doubtless have improved his answer a great deal if he had polished his English version without reference to the French original. In certain other instances there are **mis-translations** which will count heavily against the candidate; e.g. – avaient *pris congé* (=had taken leave of); – *ce qui se passait* (=what was happening); – *allait s'étendre* (=would soon be spreading); – *on vous aime bien* (=we like you a lot) and others.

Two other major areas of error are common to many candidates. The first concerns **poor English rendering of tenses**, especially **the imperfect tense**. 'Used to', 'was doing', 'would do' are all possibilities which must be examined according to the context, and the candidate must select the appropriate one for that context to gain maximum credit. *Se vidait, allait gagner* and *qui le remplissait* could all be translated better than here. The second is a recurring difficulty – the differences in the use of articles in English and French. '*The* Father Denis' sounds unnatural, and '*some* turbulent children' (i.e. not others?) is misleading.

Definite **vocabulary mistakes** (e.g. *essouflé*=breathless) and **omissions** (un *sourd* bruit) each count as a whole error, but the failure to give the exact rendering or a completely satisfactory phrase (i.e. *retentir*=to ring out) will not carry a total penalty.

Comprehension

It is easy to see from the script that the candidate's main weakness is the **transference of tense**. In question 4, for instance, the pluperfect is needed (=*la police avait trouvé*). This is both logical and in accordance with the requirements of indirect speech. The same kind of mistake recurs in questions 6 and 10. Other tense errors in questions 7 and 9 again spring from incorrect sequence of tenses (=ils ne *pourraient* pas . . . qui *serait* pleine de . . . and Max *pourrait* s'apercevoir de . . .). You should note particularly that in the second instance the use of 'pouvoir' in the conditional tense serves to indicate 'might'. Candidates are not usually familiar enough with this rendering.

The other major fault concerns the candidate's **unwillingness to stray very far from the text**. It was clearly stated earlier that this tactic is a mistaken one – how can you expect marks for mere copying from the exam paper? This criticism applies especially to questions 3, 5 and 9. You will see from the Model Answer how this kind of repetition can be avoided. In question 2 the 'lifting' of original material has actually worked against the candidate; it does not really answer the question.

If candidates do not give too much information, they give too little! In question 1 two points need to be mentioned (the rain and his hunger) and by mentioning only one the candidate has therefore lost half the possible marks.

Question 6 contains a very careless error ('que il'), an inaccuracy ('ce jour'=this very day), and an unnecessary mistake which sprang from disregard of the question (the omission of 'Je' in 'je le sais'). The question gives real help with the answer, if only the candidate were intelligent enough to look! There are also several errors due entirely to carelessness (question 7 – plei*n*; question 8 – part*irent* (past historic); question 10 – pas *des* allum*etes*). Three are copying mistakes – the candidate who throws away marks in this way is a fool! To sum up, this script is average or slightly better but it exemplifies a situation in which there are very few bonus points to balance the errors. There are only two in fact: (a) the correct manipulation of the verb 'pleuvoir' (which many others would certainly bungle), and (b) the use of the pronoun 'en' in the first phrase of question 6.

Composition

Too long – again! On the whole the essay is reasonable. Most verbs are correct although **only two tenses** are really in evidence and the **sentence structure is rather primitive**. There is certainly a weakness in the government of infinitives (e.g. 'commencer à+inf.') as well as with constructions involving the old chestnut 'dire/demander à quelqu'un de faire' (indirect object pronoun 'leur' is needed). Other pronouns are correct as regards position (a bonus) but there is some muddled thinking in the sentence 'L'autres garçons l'ont entourés'. The candidate is by no means alone in his erroneous interpretation of 'tomber' ('laisser tomber' is required), 'tourner' ('se retourner'), 'dire environ' ('parler de', etc.), 'prendre' ('emmener' – see page 83), 'le traffic' ('la circulation'). There are a few **very careless errors** (le v*ou*leur, allé *au a*gent, sur *le* route) as well as mistakes in relative pronouns and negative forms. 'Pour+inf.' is used unnecessarily with the verb 'courir'.

The squeezing in of the idiom 'sain et sauf' is not successful, because it is not clear who or what is 'safe and sound' (the bag

93

or the narrator?) and in any case sounds rather inappropriate. On the other hand the phrase 'qui est coureur' does demonstrate a linguistic point, if you are willing to accept the remarkable coincidence of having a friend on the spot who is a professional athlete! Otherwise vocabulary is undistinguished but acceptable, covering the situation adequately.

This is the only section of the examination in which the candidate may exercise any choice. This candidate has opted for what is the safest solution – concluding an incident sketched out in the question. When making your choice, consider two points carefully:
(a) Can I write a reasonable story on this subject in simple form?
(b) Do I know the essential vocabulary for writing on this topic?
Candidates rarely encounter problems with the timing of exams in this subject. Their difficulty usually lies in working at a steady pace in order to produce careful work. Following the recommended planning procedures will resolve most potential problems of this kind. After all the French exam does not demand quantity in the candidate's script; it does, however, most certainly require him to focus on the quality and accuracy of each individual element of that script.

Taking all papers into consideration, this candidate would probably be placed in the **lower range of the B grade** at O-level.

Model answers

Translation into English

Now was the time when school was emptying for three months. Children had taken leave of their teachers and families of the school's Principal. The crowd slowly coming down the staircases would reach the playground, the street, and then the station. A muffled noise kept Father Denis informed of what was happening. A vast silence would soon be spreading throughout the school, a silence which always filled him with melancholy.

At this moment the sound of galloping footsteps rang out in the corridor. The door was flung open and three pupils came in, breathlessly. It was Poussin, Le Grand and Martin. They shouted in unison, 'We've come to say a quick goodbye to you, Father Denis. See you next year! Have a good holiday! We think you're all right, you know, Father Denis' – and with that heartfelt shout, they dashed off back to their families.

Thoughtful, Father Denis was left standing all alone in front of his table. Over the course of so many years, he had seen plenty of pupils come and go. And those who had remembered him when it was time to leave had always been the same, the naughty ones like those three. The priest pondered for a moment or two. Can you really say that boisterous, waggish children are naughty, just because they are lively and impetuous? No, that would be absurd. The priest smiled, sat down again at the table, and began working.

Comprehension

1. Parce qu'il pleuvait et il avait faim.
2. Il a reconnu le signal de Jules frappé à la porte.
3. Il s'est étonné parce que, par un temps pareil, Jules ne portait ni chapeau ni imperméable et il était tard.
4. La police croyait que Jules avait volé un diamant que la femme de chambre avait trouvé dans la chambre de celui-ci.
5. Il venait demander de l'argent. Ceci a étonné Albert parce que Jules était riche et connaissait des gens riches.
6. Non, il n'en avait pas; je le sais parce que, ce jour-là, il avait acheté un livre, et donc n'a pas pu manger.
7. Il fallait en prendre une pour essayer d'éviter la police qui attendrait à la gare.
8. Après être sortis furtivement, ils sont montés dans la voiture et sont partis sans allumer les phares.
9. Il fallait retourner la voiture parce que Max pourrait remarquer son absence.
10. Il a arrêté la voiture pour examiner la boîte d'allumettes, parce qu'il n'en avait pas donné à Jules.

Composition

Si nous attendions trop longtemps, l'homme serait disparu. A ce moment-là, trois garçons forts, que je connaissais, ont tourné le coin; tout de suite je leur ai demandé de nous aider. Sans hésiter, ils ont couru après le voleur à toutes jambes. Se retournant, l'homme nous a vus qui le poursuivions. Après un quart d'heure de chasse, essouflé, il a dû s'arrêter pour reprendre haleine. Un des garçons (qui est le meilleur coureur de l'école) a réussi à rattraper le voleur. Les autres l'ont entouré pour l'empêcher de s'évader. Le sac lui est glissé des mains et je l'ai ramassé. M'approchant d'un agent qui dirigeait la circulation, je lui ai tout raconté. Bientot un fourgon a emmené le voleur en prison, et j'ai rendu le sac à la dame qui nous a remerciés chaleureusement. (*147 words*)

Other study aids in the  series

KEY FACTS CARDS

Latin
Julius Caesar
New Testament
German
Macbeth
Geography Regional
English Comprehension
English Language
Economics
Elementary Mathematics
Algebra
Modern Mathematics

English History (1815–1914)
English History (1914–1946)
Chemistry
Physics
Biology
Geometry
Geography
French
Arithmetic & Trigonometry
General Science
Additional Mathematics
Technical Drawing

KEY FACTS COURSE COMPANIONS

Economics
Modern Mathematics
Algebra
Geometry
Arithmetic & Trigonometry
Additional Mathematics

Geography
French
Physics
Chemistry
English
Biology

KEY FACTS A-LEVEL BOOKS

Chemistry
Biology

Pure Mathematics
Physics

KEY FACTS O-LEVEL PASSBOOKS

Modern Mathematics
Geography
Biology
Chemistry
Economics

Physics
English History (1815–1939)
French
English

KEY FACTS O-LEVEL MODEL ANSWERS

Modern Mathematics
Geography
Biology
Chemistry

Physics
English History (1815–1939)
French
English

KEY FACTS REFERENCE LIBRARY

O–Level Biology
O–Level Physics
O–Level Chemistry

O–Level Trad. & Mod. Maths
O–Level Geography
O–Level English History (1815–1914)

KEYFACTS A–LEVEL PASSBOOKS

Physics
Biology
Geography
Economics

Chemistry
Pure Maths
Pure & Applied Mathematics
Applied Mathematics